DISCARD

AMERICAN WOMEN
images and realities

AMERICAN WOMEN
Images and Realities

Advisory Editors
ANNETTE K. BAXTER
LEON STEIN

A Note About This Volume

The spinster Smith sisters, Abby Hadassah (1797-1878) and Julia Evelina (1792-1886) lived a quiet life of learning, good works and husbandry on their farm in Glastonbury, Connecticut, until 1869, when, hit by a double tax, they raised a cry for representation and joined the fight for suffrage and women's rights. Another tax in 1872, directed especially at women, caused these sprightly ancient warriors to make soapbox speeches in town and to take to the courts, even while their land and their cattle were being confiscated by the town fathers. They fought and won their case while the whole world watched, laughed and learned.

ABBY SMITH 𝔞𝔫𝔡 HER COWS

BY
MISS JULIA E. SMITH

ARNO PRESS
A New York Times Company
New York • 1972

Reprint Edition 1972 by Arno Press Inc.

American Women: Images and Realities
ISBN for complete set: 0-405-04445-3
See last pages of this volume for titles.

Manufactured in the United States of America

– – – – – – – – – – – – –

Library of Congress Cataloging in Publication Data

Smith, Julia E   1792-1886.
    Abby Smith and her cows.

    (American women: images and realities)
    Reprint of the 1877 ed.
    1. Women--Rights of women. 2. Women in the United
States. I. Title. II. Series.
HQ1426.S59 1972   301.41'2'0973   72-2622
ISBN 0-405-04478-X

ABBY SMITH AND HER COWS

ABBY SMITH AND HER COWS.

ABBY SMITH AND HER COWS

WITH A

REPORT OF THE LAW CASE

DECIDED CONTRARY TO LAW.

BY
MISS JULIA E. SMITH.

HARTFORD, CONN.
1877.

ABBY SMITH'S COWS.

There were seven cows in all, at the first sale at the Sign-post. Of these, three have since been disposed of. The four others represented in the frontispiece—named Daisy, Whitey, Minnie, and Proxy, with one other, have been driven to be sold at the Auction Block, this Centennial year; a fine commentary on the doings of our Forefathers a hundred years ago. One of the calves represented, belongs to proxy, and came while the mother was shut up to be forced to the Sign-post, and was named Martha Washington, by a young friend and near neighbor, shortly before her death. The other calf is Whitey's, and is called Abigail Adams.

JULIA E. SMITH.

July 31st, 1876.

INTRODUCTION.

Perhaps the public would like to learn the cirumstances which first led two defenceless women, to make such a stand as they have done against taxation without representation.

They were quiet peaceable citizens of the town of Glastonbury, Ct., born and brought up there, having no idea of going contrary to men's laws, neither have they by any means broken one of them. Without any fault of their own, have they been driven into their present unpleasant situation.

The first time I ever said anything in self-defence to any of the town officers was in 1869. An overseer of the highway called here in June, and brought a bill of about eighteen dollars and said it was not due till fall, but wished we would furnish the money beforehand, for he must pay the laborers and could get no money from the men. I paid it, and the next October there was another highway tax sent in of about the same amount. I thought there must be a mistake, and did not want to pay it over twice. I called on the overseer, but he seemed to know nothing how it happened. He was a republican and wanted to give me some insight into town affairs, and show me how miserably the democrats governed the town, and got the late town report to read to me. I told him I knew not how to stay, and I had no power to help it. But he read several items and among the rest was more than $700 for registering men's names. "What's that?" said I. "Why there has been a law passed, which I approve ; for some men would vote twice over if their names were not put down." "But who pays this?" "Why the tax payers of course." "But if I wanted my name set down would they do it?" "Oh no! it is the voter's names." "What! and make the women pay for it?" He said the democrats charged a third more than the republicans, for the democrats charged three dollars a day, horse hire and a dinner. "And then make the women pay for it? If they are going on at this rate, I must go to that suffrage meeting in Hartford and see if we cannot do better, for I have no doubt one woman would write down every name in town for half that money."

To the suffrage meeting we went, the day but one after. It was presided over by Dr. Burton, and capital speeches were made. Snow on the ground, travelling bad, a raw, sour day ; we could stay at only one session, and came home believing that the women had truth on their side ; but never did it once enter our heads to refuse to pay taxes.. Not long after we had sickness and death in the family, and lost our eldest sister, the life of the house, who had a keen sense of injustice. In 1872 when Collector Cornish called for our taxes, (not collector Andrews the cow auctioneer.) I asked him why our assessment was more than last year, for we laid up no money and did not intend to. He replied, the assessor had a right to add to our tax as much as he pleased, and he had assessed our house and homestead a hundred dollars more. To be sure it increased our tax but little, but what is unjust in least is unjust in much. I inquired if it was done so to any man's property. He looked over his book to see, and not a man had his tax raised; there were only two widows in our neighborhood that were so used. I told him how wrong it was to treat us in this manner, for we could not even raise money enough from our land to pay its taxes, but men had strength and could raise tobacco and pay theirs readily. He said he would see the selectmen and call again. He did call again with peremptory orders to collect it, and that year we paid over $200 to the town. That man was killed the next winter by being thrown out of his sleigh against a post near his own door. Had he lived, I do not believe he would ever been forced by any authority to use us so outrageously as collector Andrews has done.

My sister who has the most courage of the two, and seemed to think almost the whole of our native town friendly to us, declared she was not going to be so unjustly used, without telling of it. I warned her of the consequences, and as we had so short a time to stay here, we had better submit; and asked how she would do it? She said, when the men met in town meeting. I at last consented to go with her to the town hall, she having written better than I thought possible. My scrap book entitled "Abby Smith and her Cows," must give the sequel.

I have not taken half the comments of the newspapers sent us from more than two hundred offices in these United States. Instead of a pamphlet, the book might have increased into quite a volume. As women have no redress only to tell their wrongs, even courts deciding contrary to law for fear of offending voters, I hope this pamphlet may be favorably received by a discerning public.

JULIA E. SMITH.

GLASTONBURY, CT., Sept. 16th 1876.

Why Miss Abby H. Smith Objected to Pay Taxes,

AND THE RESULT.

From the *Springfield Republican, Dec.*
11th, 1873.

A NOVEL SPEECH FOR A TOWN MEETING.

The argument for woman suffrage was put before the farmers of Glastonbury, at their town meeting, last week, in a way that can hardly have failed to make some impression upon them. Among the tax-payers of that town are two maiden sisters by the name of Smith, whose father was a prominent citizen, a generation ago, doing all the law business of that place for nearly 40 years. Dying, he left his farm to his daughters, and the taxes on it that were formerly assessed upon him have since been paid by them. Probably, scarcely one of the farmers who have regularly assembled in town meetings to vote the taxes for the ensuing year ever had the idea enter his head that the Misses Smith might possibly feel a slight degree of interest in the levying of those taxes, from the fact that they were required to pay between one and two hundred dollars of the total amount. Very likely they would have gone on with similar thoughtlessness in future but for a rather peculiar incident that characterized their town meeting, last Wednesday. That incident was the appearance of the Misses Smith, and a speech by one of them. Miss Abby H. Smith, which was a very creditable address for a woman who has not devoted herself to public speaking.

From the *Hartford Courant.*

SPEECH OF MISS ABBY H. SMITH,
Of Glastonbury, before the Town Meeting
of that place November 5th, 1873.

It is not without due deliberation that we have been willing to attend this meeting, but we had no other way of coming before the men of the town. Others, our neighbours, can complain more effectually than we can, without speaking a word, when they think those who rule over them rule with injustice ; but we are not put under the laws of the land as they are—we are wholly in the power of those we have come to address. You have the power over our property to take it from us whenever you chose, and we can have no voice in the matter whatever, not even to say what shall be done with it, and no power to appeal to; we are perfectly defenseless. Can you wonder, then, we should wish to speak with you? People do not generally hold power without exercising it, and those who exercise it do not appear to have the least idea of its injustice. The Southern slaveholder only possessed the same power that you have to rule over us. "Happy dog," he would say of his slave, "I have given him everything; I am the slave, and he the master; does he complain? give him ten lashes." The slaveholder really thought they had done so much for their slaves they would not leave them, when the great consideration was, the slave wanted the control of his own earnings; and so does every human being of what rightfully belongs to him. We do not suppose the men of the town think they have done so much for us that they have a right to take our money when they please. But then there is always excuse enough where there is power. They say all the property of the town should be taxed for the expenses of the town, according to its valuation, and as taxation without representation is wrong, they give permission to a part of these owners to say what valuation shall be made, and how the money can best be applied for their benefit. They meet together to consult who among them shall have the offices of the town and what salary they will give them. All is this done without ever consulting or alluding to the other part of the owners of this property. But they tax the other owners and take from them just what amount they please. We had two hundred dollars taken from us in this way the past year, by the same power the robber takes his money, because we are defenceless and cannot resist. But the robber would have the whole community against him, and he would not be apt to come but once; but from the men of our town we are never safe—they can come in and take our money from us.

just when they choose. Now, we cannot see any justice, any right, or any reason in this thing. We cannot see why we are not just as capable of assisting in managing the affairs of the town as the men are. We cannot possibly see why we have not just as much intelligence and information or as much capacity for doing business, as they have. Are we not as far-seeing, and do we not manage our own affairs, as far as we are permitted by the laws, as well as they do? Is it any more just to take a woman's property without her consent, than it is to take a man's property without his consent? Those whom the town put over us are the very dregs of society, those who are making the town and their families continual expense and trouble, for which we are liable, and the authorities make the town pay the expense of meeting to take off their poll tax, for they can't pay a dollar; and they have taken some from the insane retreat and kept them in a barn over night to vote the next day. Now all these things clearly prove how much more these lawless men are valued by the town than such citizens as we are, who never make it the least trouble or expense. Such men as these are set over us and can vote away our property; indeed, our property is liable to their support. Now all we ask of the town is to put us on an equality with these men, not to rule over them as they rule over us, but to be put on an equality with them. Is this an unreasonable request? Do we not stand on an equality with them, and every man in this assembly with them, and every man in this assembly and every man in this God is a God of justice; men and women stand alike in his sight; he has but one law for both. And why should man have but one law for both, to which both shall be accountable alike? Let each rise if they can by their own ability, and put no obstructions in their way. Is it right because men are the strongest, that they should go into the women's houses and take their money from them, knowing they cannot resist? It is not physical strength that makes a town prosper; it is mind; it is capability to guide the physical strength and put its resources to the best possible advantage. You are rejecting just half of the very element you need. You well know that a man and his wife must counsel together to make the affairs of their household prosper; they must be one in the business, and if they are one, I cannot see how one can rule over the other, from which idea comes all the disturbance between them. Ought not this town to represent one great family all equally interested in its government? As it is, its government is no concern of ours whatever. We cannot alter it if we see ever so much injustice.

No woman concerns herself about the government of the town, being placed under the men, instead of being placed under the laws, their whole business is to please the men as the slave's business is to please his master, because their living comes from the men; the laws are such that they can get in no other way. The motto of our government is "Proclaim liberty to all the inhabitants of the land," and here where liberty is so highly extolled and gloried by every man in it, one-half the inhabitants are not put under her laws, but are ruled over by the other half, who can by their own laws, not hers, take from the other half all they possess. How is Liberty pleased with such worship? Would she not be apt to think of her own sex?

This assembly have put such men as Judge Hunt over us, to fine a woman one hundred dollars for doing what is an honor for a man to do, and denied us a trial by jury. This is the highest court in the land made by your votes. No man ever had more regard for this town than our father had. He was born and brought up here, and all his ancestors before him. He knew every man in it, and seemed as much interested in their welfare as his own. He was a man that any town would be proud of. He did all its law business for nearly forty years. Did he ever take any of its money without giving full compensation? It was never said of him. Is not this the great law of nations, that compensation shall be made when money is taken from women as well as men? But instead of compensation it is taken from us and every other woman in the place, to strengthen the power of those that rule over us. It is taken to pay the men for making laws to govern us, by which they themselves would not be governed under any consideration. Neither would we, if we could help it. Some of it is given to buy votes which add to their power. A man's wife told me they gave her husband four dollars, which kept him drunk a long time to abuse his family. His wife said if she could vote, her vote would be as good as her husband's, and the men which came after him to carry him to the polls would treat her as well as they treated him. Her hard earnings could not be taken for his drams. And some of the money is taken for the authorities of the town to meet at all the different hotels in it, to make voters and take off the poll tax of all the poor vagabonds, that they may vote; then the authorities want to meet to consult what would be most for the advantage of half of the inhabitants of the town, who do the business and put them into office (the women are not mentioned, of course, for having no power they are of no consequence) and then these officers are furnished with an entertainment at the expense of all the inhabitants of the town. But the roads make the most complaint to every woman that owns property; they all know as well as we do, that they would not be made as they are before their houses if they could vote. We have every reason to think the officers of the town add what they please to our taxes. Last year they added $100 to our homestead without giving us any notice, and the same amount to two widows in the neighborhood, who cannnot work their land, and not a man who can work it had his property raised, for he could find it out and a woman could not.

We have paid the town of Glastonbury during the last six years more than $1000, and for what? to be ruled over and be put under, what all the citizens know to be the lowest and worthless of any in the place. We ask only for ourselves and our property. Why should we be cast out? Why should we be outlawed? We should be glad to stay in our homestead where we were born and have always lived, the little time we have to stay, and to be buried with our family and ancestors, but its pleasantness is gone, for we know we do not hold it in security as our neighbors hold theirs; that it is liable to be taken from us whenever the town sees fit.

The town collector called for our taxes on Monday at sunset—the last day and hour he could call. We told him we would prefer to wait till we had been heard by the town, for if they gave us no hopes of voting, we wanted them to sell our farm for the taxes, for it was but reasonable, if they owned it, to get the taxes from it, we could not; and we wished they would begin at the east end and come into the street, for we wanted to save our homestead while we lived, and thought it would last us. He said he hoped he should not be the collector then. He agreed to all the injustice of which we complained.

From the Hartford Courant.

A LETTER FROM ABBY H. SMITH AND SISTER.

Many persons who read the above speech of Miss Smith, wanted to hear what came of it. To answer these in the readiest way, Miss S. wrote the following letter:—

To the Editor of the Courant:

Several having read my speech in your paper have requested to know how it was received by the town, and if you would publish the sequel I should feel greatly obliged. The collector called a second time this evening, as we had told him our paying the tax depended entirely upon the encouragement we received about voting,

after adressing the meeting. We told him to-night we received none at all. We thought no man had spoken about it, for what could they say? The facts must be admitted, and their not speaking cf them showed they did not intend that we should vote. Now what would you do? Mr. A., said we, if some men should get together and agree that you should pay them a certain sum, every little while, without your consent, and without your having the least advantage by it; would you pay it, or would you let them get it as they could? This is precisely our case; there is no difference between us; it is just as wrong to take it from us as it is to take it from you. Therefore we had come to the conclusion, if the town owned our farm (about 130 acres) it belonged to the men to get out of it what they said we should pay, for *we* never could; and it surely did not belong to us to assist them in any way, having no voice in the matter.

As to the expense of selling it off, it made no difference to us by what name they called it, expense or anything else, so long as they could take the whole. Our money we owned, and we were not willing, any more, to take what we owned to pay for what we did not own. Our father, when he advised us to keep the farm, said, "You need not cultivate it, but it wont run away from you." It did not seem to enter his mind but what we might hold it as securely as the men held theirs; but, being a lawyer he must have known that as soon as he died it would pass into the hands of the men of the town, and not be secured to us by the laws of the land, as the men hold their property. The collector enquired if we wished to begin at the east end first (the farm is three miles long and twenty-two and a half rods wide). We said we would be glad to save our homestead, while we lived, but then our homestead did not look so well to us as it did when we thought we owned it. The movable property would not go very far, for we believed they must leave us, as they did to the poor man, one cow and its keeping, and a part of our furniture. Mr. A., the collector, said, as many do, he thought women that had property ought to vote. We said those that had none needed it more. If they could have the power to vote against the grog shops, their drunken husbands would never dare to abuse them as they did, but they could do it now with impunity, for the town officers would not punish a voter; women have no redress for whatever injury they may receive from a voter! If the women could have voted, the town would never have been so in debt. It is very hard for them to earn their money, and they are more careful whom they trust, and would never have employed those men who have brought in such enormous bills against the town.

We inquired of the collector if there were any in the place that are taxed higher than we are. We knew of one that was, but never paid any money; he took much more from the town than he paid it. The collector mentioned but one other that was taxed higher, but said he had orders on the town to pay. Of course they have orders on the town to pay—those that rule—and many work out their taxes on the roads, bridges, etc., and then there is a rotation in office that gives them all a chance at the money, which is taken mostly from the women. The town is six miles on the river and eight miles east from the river, seven miles from Hartford. And now, if my sister and I pay the highest taxes, in money, of any of the inhabitants of this large place, how does it look as to the administration of its justice? The town is doubtless managed like our school districts in which we pay the highest tax, double to any of· the men but one. The voters decided a few years ago to have a new schoolhouse, and a contractor offered to build it for the same price he had just finished one a few miles off. But the men rejected the offer, for they said they wanted to work out their taxes, which they did, and more too, charging what they pleased to the district, which made the expense to the women nearly as much again as what the contractor offered to do the whole for. There is not a man but what knows it is perfectly just and right for us to have the same protection, under the laws, that he has; neither does he fear Judge Hunt, but it is hard to give up power. Some of them mention the Catholics, forgetting that all the command which is given to man is, "Do justly." God alone controls the consequences. The collector said, when he left, that he should call again.

ABBY H. SMITH AND SISTER.

Glastonbury, Nov. 29, 1873

From the Springfield Republican.

SMITH, THE WOMAN AND TAX-PAYER, AGAIN.

A few weeks ago, we called the attention of our readers to a rather notable speech that had just been delivered in a town meeting at Glastonbury. Ct. The speaker was Miss Abby H. Smith, a maiden lady, who spoke for herself and her sister, the representatives of one of the oldest and best families in the town, and together paying about the largest tax assessed on any of the three thousand inhabitants. Her speech was a demand for a voice in the voting of that tax, and was supported with an earnestness and force that made it quite impressive

reading. After putting before her audience the bare facts in the case, and the grounds of simple justice upon which the two sisters asked merely to be "put on an equality with the men," this new speaker at Glastonbury town meetings concluded by announcing the decision at which they had arrived before going to the meeting. This was, that, if they were given no hope of voting, the town must sell the farm their father had left them for the taxes, "for it was but reasonable, if they owned it, to get the taxes from it—we could not."

There was such power in the plain statement, of their demand that no male tax-payer had the hardihood to attempt an answer, and the routine business of the meeting was resumed where it had been dropped to give Miss Smith a hearing, no action whatever being taken with reference to the subject. Matters have since remained *in statu quo* and a few days ago, when the tax-collector called a second time for the $200 assessed upon the women, his first vist having been made shortly before the town meeting. He didn't get the money but he did get a catechism which must have been rather disagreeable, and the report of which ought to furnish matter for serious thought to such men in Glastonbury as have any sense of justice. The Misses Smith asked him if there were any persons in the town taxed higher than they are; he could mention but one, and that man has orders on the town to pay, while the women, of course, are required to pay cash down. Further, these inquisitive women put this practical interrogatory to Mr. Collector: "What would you do if some men should get together and agree that you should pay them a certain sum, every little while, without your consent, and without your having the least advantage by it,—would you pay it, or would you let them get it as they could?" After a little more plain talk in this vein, the women told the tax-gatherer that they had come to this conclusion; "If the town owns our farm (about 130 acres), it belongs to the men to get out of it what they say we shall pay, for *we* never could, and it surely does not belong to us to assist them, in any way, having no voice in the matter." Finding that this was their ultimatum, the puzzled collector left with the statement that he would "call again."

We are heartily glad that the Misses Smith have taken this position. It brings into sharper relief the injustice of denying women the right to vote than any number of speeches on woman suffrage in the abstract. That these two women, paying into the town treasury more money every year than any man in the place, should have absolutely no voice in the disposition of that money simply because they are women, is a state of things so utterly opposed to every sentiment of fair-play, that we are glad the men of Glastonbury—and of every other New England town—are thus practically confronted with the inherent absurdity and injustice of their attitude.

From the *Springfield Republican, Jan. 6th,* 1874.

ABBY SMITH'S COWS.

TAXATION WITHOUT REPRESENTATION.

WHAT MALE GLASTONBURY DID ON NEW-YEAR'S DAY.

AN IDYL OF MODERN NEW ENGLAND.

GLASTONBURY, January 3, 1874.
To the Editor of the Republican :—
The collector called again, New-year's day, and I will give you the result. We told him we were glad to see him—more so, we thought, than any of the women; for he was a sensible man and could see into the injustice of this business, more than half the town's officers.

We had no idea, then, that he had brought an attachment with him to execute it that very day, for he had always before told us we might let the tax be, as long as we pleased, by paying 12 per cent interest. But now, he said, the law must be executed, and, as he must take personal property first, our cows would be driven away at once unless his bill was settled. This came suddenly upon us, and we told him we were very sorry; more sorry for Mr. K. and his family, who lived in our cottage, than for ourselves, for we could do without the milk better than they could. We have a fine lot of Alderneys that my sister had raised, every one, for amusement, and cared for, and was much attached to them. We pleaded hard for a respite, till we could speak again before the town. We wanted to petition the men, we said, to let us own our land as they owned theirs, and then we would willingly pay our taxes; and how much better it would be to have the money paid freely than to have all this trouble about it! The town had waited on a factory company in the north part of the place for their taxes for years, till the company failed, and they lost several thousand dollars by it. We had our share of this money to pay; a larger share, as it appeared by his books, than any other of the inhabitants, and there was no risk in waiting for us to pay. But they were men, and we are women.

"Now," said we "Mr. A., you would not be willing personally to take a woman's property because she cannot vote to defend it; no other man in town would; though you will agree together to do it. But numbers can never make it right; no reckoning can prove it." My sister went into the yard to entreat him to leave two of the cows together (there were eight of them) that one might not be left alone. But she could not prevail, and the little thing, the poor man's portion, has cried ever since. He took seven, for he said cows were low and he wanted enough! The tax now is only $101.39. The next tax comes in March.

The cows were taken to a neighbor's, some little distance, and my sister felt very bad all night, thinking how they might fare, and requested Mr. H., early in the morning, to see to them, for he understands how to manage them better than any one ever before. The neighbor said nothing could excede the trouble they had to get them into his yard (for it seems they resisted, every way they could), and he would never had it done had he known the circumstances, or that they were to stay over night. He could do nothing with them, and requested Mr. K. to milk them for him. These cows will sometimes be very contrary, when nobody can manage them but my sister. She will call them all by their names, and as soon as they hear, they will come to her upon the gallop. They will follow behind her in single file, and she can lead them wherever she chooses. When we have had a new tenant they would never, at first, let him come near them, and she has been obliged to stand at their head, where they could see her, every day, when he milked, for ever so long.

Yesterday, we went to Hartford, seven miles, to see our lawyer, so that neither we nor the other should transgress. The sale is to take place next Thursday. 'Tis rather hard, in the depth of winter, for women to be obliged to attend an auction sale of their own cows. I will try to give you an account of it. They are to be driven a half mile to the sign-post. Our lawyer said there was no need for this severity now, as the tax was perfectly safe.

ABBY H. SMITH.

We ask every thoughtful man who has the ballot, and every thoughtless woman who is in the habit of saying she doesn't want it, to read Abby Smith's story of the New-year's call paid her by the tax-collector of Glastonbury. It is well worth reading, if only for the quaint simplicity of the style. This is a bit of Defoe's English, ladies and gentlemen. But the matter is still more noteworthy than the manner, and it is to this that we particularly want to direct your attention.

In refusing to continue paying heavier taxes, year by year, than any other property-owners in Glastonbury, while refused a voice in assessing and spending them, Abby Smith and her sister as truly stand for the American principle as did the citizens who ripped open the tea-chests in Boston harbor, or the farmers who leveled their muskets at Concord. And they seem to have very much the same quality of quiet, old-fashioned Yankee grit, too. They are not demonstrative or declamatory. They don't shriek, or wring their hands, or make a fuss of any sort. They are good-nature itself. But they are also logic itself, and resolution itself, and pluck itself. They simply stand upon their rights. Satisfied of the , strength of their position, they content themselves with opposing to legalized injustice that passive resistance which is sometimes the hardest of all to overcome. It is rather a fine spectacle when you come to think of it, and withal a very suggestive one.

It will not be creditable either to the hearts and heads of the woman-suffrage party if Abby Smith and her sister are left to stand alone—to fight this battle of principle unaided. That party numbers in its ranks justly distinguished lawyers; we could mention one or two who live within an hour's ride of Glastonbury. It also numbers a great many men and women of wealth. Here is a chance for them to prove their faith by their works; they are not likely to have, as they could not well ask, a better one. And, in these matters, "chance" is a synonym for "duty." We submit that subscribing to the Abby Smith Defense Fund is the first business in order.

From the Springfield Republican, Jan. 12th, 1874.

GLASTONBURY, AGAIN.

THE MAJESTY OF THE LAW VINDICATED.

ABBY SMITH DESCRIBES THE SALE OF HER COWS.

To the Editor of the Republican:—

GLASTONBURY, CT., January 8, 1874.

This day has witnessed a transaction never before seen in this town or in any other, I am sure, in all New England.

We walked, at noon, two or three houses above us to see the cattle let out of their pen. By orders of the collector, the cows —seven of them—had been huddled into a space of 15 feet by 12 (measured by my sister) and tied up for seven days and

rights, together; always having had their freedom before. It was a tobacco-shed, and the owner had to bring them hay from another building, and give them water from pails, drawn from a well at some distance. We saw twenty-one pails-full carried at one day. He did the best he could under the circumstances. The collector could not have let them out, well knowing that it would take the whole authority of the town to ever confine them there again. Mr. K., our tenant, had to take the milk, for the sensitive young wife of the tobacco-shed owner declared that a drop of that milk should never come into her house, for it seemed to her just as if it was stolen. Mrs. K. said, yesterday, that the cows had failed, by two-thirds, of their milk since they were taken from our yard.

The procession soon started, headed by the collector (who is also constable), leading the best cow; the others, driven by four men with a dog and a drum; several teams; and we in the rear in a wagon with Mr. and Mrs. K. We intended to walk together alone, but Mr. K. insisted upon our riding, as his wife was determined to go with us. Mrs. K. remarked on the way that it appeared like a funeral. There were about 40 men at the sign-post, who bid so low that Mr. K. was forced to speak for the four best, below their value, which covered the tax and expenses, leaving the three smallest. All would have been sacrificed, for it was evident from the bids that they intended to get them for a song. Not a man came to speak to us. It was remarked by one who liked the business that the whole town was against us. We thought we had many friends as we have been treated with the greatest outward respect, as if we were complete, with only one failing,—that of not paying our taxes, this winter. We would not have believed the town could thus persecute women who were born and bred here, among the oldest and most law abiding of its citizens, who have never refrained from visiting the sick and distressed throughout the whole town, watching through long nights in hovels where none was willing to enter; and those too, who have paid the most money into the town's treasury. We understand there is due $2000 for taxes from voters, who are released by paying 12 per cent interest, and we pleaded for the same indulgence; but we were women, and had no power. It will not do to offend a voter.

We know not what they will do when the March tax is claimed, but must not now be surprised at anything. They say personal estate must be seized first, and we greatly fear they will ransack our house, tear up our carpets, and take ornamental things, the work of a lamented sister, and her fine paintings,—for she was an artist. My sister says her feelings will not be so much tried as by the sufferings of her cows. She has interested herself in sedentary pursuits, having translated and written out the whole Bible, three times, with her own hand, from the Hewbrew, Greek and Latin, and needs out-door exercise. She says now she can no more have the comfort of raising a fine calf, now and then, from the dread of following it to the sign-post to see it sacrificed. We are now in a lonely situation. We were long a family of five sisters; we are now but two. . As the town now manages our property, we must soon be forced to the poor-house, and none are better acquainted with its inmates.

The town's answer to all this will be, "Pay your taxes, then,"—the same answer the British gave to our Revolutionary ancestors.   ABBY H. SMITH.

From the Boston Daily Advertiser, Jan. 13th, 1874.

GLASTONBURY AFFAIRS.

Two Connecticut women are just now doing a mightier work in behalf of their sex, or that portion of it which has a taste for public affairs, than all the rest in the country. Abby H. Smith and her sister live in Glastonbury, a town heretofore without notable prestige. They own a farm and manage it creditably. The pecularity of their case is, if we take their statement, that in the apportionment of taxes they have been treated with great unfairness. Being without the ballot, the most serviceable weapon of protest, their fellow-citizens of the other sex have as rashly as ungallantly extorted from them a disproportionate share of taxation. And not only have they done this, but they have refused to permit them to share equally with other citizens in the benefits accruing from expenditure of the public money in road improvements, etc. Wherefore Miss Abby Smith and her sister went to the last town meeting, and one of them, having asked and obtained leave to make a statement to the voters assembled, did, in a dignified, moderate and reasonable way, set forth the facts of their oppression by taxation while representation was denied, and respectfully asked that inasmuch as they were the largest taxpayers in the town, and had shown, by lives of successful industry, their capacity for business, they might be allowed to vote with the other taxpayers on the subjects considered in town meeting. Her short speech was reported at the time, and it certainly did not offend in any point of decorum or reasoning. The conclusion of their statement was that if the town persisted in its course of preying upon their property and applying it to the advantage of others, refusing them any voice in the matter, the town would be obliged to take possession of the farm, as they could not themselves conduct it profitably. The address was quietly listened to, and its suggestions were scrupulously ignored.

So the matter rested. The Misses Smith declined to pay their winter tax, in accordance with their declared purpose. They were told, it seems, that it could remain unpaid as long as they chose to have it do so, they paying interest on it at the rate of 12 per cent., that being a custom of the town. But subsequently the town authorities grew restive at the idea of being resisted by two women, or perhaps the failure to collect the large sum levied upon the sisters embarrassed the treasury. Although there was due the town a large amount of uncollected taxes from men and voters who preferred to retain the principal by paying interest, it could not be tolerated that the same favor should be shown to women, who were not voters. On New Year's day the collector called with an attachment, and seized and drove off seven of a herd of eight Alderney cows which one of the sisters had raised, to satisfy his bill for $101.39. The collector appears to have magnified his office and shown an unnecessary hardness of heart. When entreated to leave two cows that they might be company for each other, he refused, and the one left moaned all night in her loneliness. Cows are not commonly so sentimental, but these were a woman's cows. Moreover they had been cossetted and trained by their mistress to that degree that while they were very good cows to her they were quite "contrary" in their behavior toward strangers. She could call each by its name and it would come to her galloping. All would follow her in single file wherever she led. The man who milked them had a rough experience in the beginning, for they would not suffer him to do so for weeks, except their mistress stood by to give assurance that the attempt had her countenance, so to speak. The tax-collector had a troublesome time driving them to a neighbor's and impounding them in his yard. Nor was that the end of vexations, for when they were secured the man to whose manipulations they were accustomed had to be sent for to milk them. On Thursday last the cows were sold. The story of the auction is a pathetic one, and we despair of telling it better than one of the sisters has done in a letter given in another column.

In a previous communication to the same journal Miss Smith says: "We pleaded hard for a respite till we could speak again before the town. We wanted to petition the men, we said, to let us own our land as they owned theirs, and then we would willingly pay our taxes. . . . The town had waited on a factory company in the north part of the place for their taxes for years, till the company failed, and they lost several thousand dollars by it. We had our share of this money to pay; a larger share, as it appeared by his books, than any other of the inhabitants, and there was no risk in waiting for us to pay. But they were men and we are women." The statement we have is, to be sure, *ex parte*, but there is no reason to think it unfair. There can hardly be a question but that the town officers have made up their minds to suppress the passive resistance of these women to being plundered of their possessions. Perhaps they will succeed, but they have undertaken a task that promises to be wearisome before it is accomplished. The fame of their contest with women is certain to go abroad, and it behooves them if they regard their good names, to refrain from all unnecessary harshness. The case on the part of the women is about as strong as it could be. They are confessedly intelligent, industrious and capable of managing their affairs. They own in their own right the property which is taxed, and manage it independently. They are freer than most male voters from the incumbrance of domestic bonds, nor can it be said that they are represented by anybody else whose interests and sympathies are indentical with theirs.

From the Springfield Republican, Jan. 14th 1874.

THAT FUND.

The time seems to have come for " talking business," as the slang of the day has it. A note which has just reached us will serve very well as text:—

To the Editor of the Republican:—

I take five dollars worth of stock in the Glaston bury Smith sisters "Defense Fund." I believe it will pay. Inclosed you will find the stamps. In haste.   JAMES NOBLE, JR.

Westfield, Mass., January 12, 1874.

The first suggestion of this fund came from The Republican—not from the Misses Smith. It was as novel a suggestion to them as to any other two readers who found it in their morning papers. They had not then, and have not since, asked any one for a penny. They are not, in any sense, objects of charity, and any money sent to them in the way of alms would be pretty sure to find its way back to the sender's pocket by return mail. It is not a question of charity, at all; it is a question of justice. The contest in which these women have so pluckily embarked is not a personal contest, but a contest of principle. They are fighting the

fight of an entire sex and of a great cause. They are doing this against formidable odds. They have already sustained damage in pocket and feelings; they are likely to sustain more. It seemed to us very unjust that these women should be allowed to go to this war at their own charges. It seemed only proper and fair that the wealthier friends of the cause and members of the sex for which they are doing such good work, should assure them against pecuniary loss; more than that, should provide the sinews of war for a sharp and thoroughly-fought campaign. Hence our suggestion.

From the Springfield Republican, Jan. 15th 1874.

THE EXACT ISSUE AT GLASTONBURY.

Whether the taxes assessed upon Abby Smith and her sister are, in fact, excessive, is a question by itself. So is the question whether they have been unjustly discriminated against in the expenditure of the town's money; and the other question whether, if they had had votes, they would have fared better in either particular. These problems are of more interest to the Misses Smith than to the public, and the logic and rhetoric brought to their solution by some of our cotemporaries must be set down as a sad waste of uncommonly fine raw intellectual material.

We don't mean, if we can help it, to allow the real issue here, the issue in which the public *is* interested, to be whisked out of sight under cover of a fog of irrelevant discussion. This issue is perfectly simple; the wayfaring man, though a fool, can't honestly pretend that he doesn't understand it, when it is once put before him. Abby Smith and her sister have paid in more money to the town treasury of Glastonbury than any of their neighbors. They have had absolutely no voice in deciding how much money should be raised, or to what uses it should be put after it was raised. Some women who hold property in their own right are " constructively " represented in town meetings and at the polls by a male relative—father, brother, or husband, as the case may be. But these women are not even " constructively " represented; their disfranchisement has been complete and absolute. They now demand as a right that this disfranchisement shall cease; that they shall be given, in future, an equal voice with their neighbors and townsmen in assessing and expending the town taxes. Is this demand just, or is it not? Is taxation without representation, which was wrong at Boston in 1774, right at Glastonbury in 1874? This is the issue forced upon the intelligent, justice-loving people of Connecticut by the refusal of these two women to longer pay taxes under the existing conditions.

This bare statement of the issue effectually disposes of the suggestion that, if these women found their taxes too heavy, they should have appealed to the courts. The other suggestion that, as long as the law is what it is, they should have obeyed it, contenting themselves with petitioning for its modification, reads very queerly in the columns of a New England newspaper. How about certain acts of Parliament toward the close of the last century? How about the fugitive-slave act?

From the Hartford Daily Times, Jan. 14th, 1874.

"ABBY SMITH'S COWS."

[The following letter from an esteemed lady friend goes wide of the mark, and overlooks the actual state of the case; but its sincerity entitles it to respect:—]

WHICH IS HIGHEST, LAW OR JUSTICE?

December 16, 1773, a party of men, disguised as Indians, went on board some vessels in Boston Harbor, and threw their cargoes overboard. No one ever claimed that the act was in accordance with law, but it has been cited as an instance where man's love of justice overcame his respect for law.

Now, may I ask, how the action of the Misses Smith, in refusing to submit to being taxed without being represented, differs, in spirit, from that of 1773, which has been highly commended?

If "Resistance to tyrants is obedience to God," why is it not as honorable for a woman to resist injustice, in her own chosen way, as it is for a man?

There is no question of minors or idiots in this, but one of woman's right to self-government; and why men should fear to grant that right which they consider their highest privilege, to women, while declaring that not one woman in five hundred would exercise her right to the franchise, is a mystery. If the suffrage should bring upon women all the evils which men predict, are women so devoid of wit as to retain a right which has proved injurious to them? Why not tell the truth? Say. "We want our slaves to remain as they are, forever." You will never do that. Men prefer to cry "Great is Diana of the Ephesians," when the secret thought of their hearts is, "Our craft is in danger." So you cry up "law and order," while dooming others, in no way inferior to yourselves, to a life that no law would make you endure for one year. For the foreign tyrant one can rebel against, but when, like the frogs of Egypt, he pervades the house—bellows in the pulpit — swarms in the courts of justice, and makes the laws that he alone can repeal, one does

not wonder that under such tyranny slaves should deteriorate.

There was no talk of the inferiority of women during the Revolution; nor would there be now, if women had the right to help make the laws she must obey. Before the Revolution the women and men in America were governed alike—but by a superior class.

The Misses Smith have only asked to be placed upon an equality—that is claimed by the great bill of rights, the Declaration of Independence, as the inalienable right of all humanity,—with the meanest man who is a voter in their native town.

They have not asked that they may, by advantage of wealth, education or purity of life, be given the power to make laws for ignorant or indigent men. They wish all to be equal before the law, as all are equal before God.

What has been done here in Glastonbury that requires explanation from men? Two American ladies considering a law unjust, refused to comply with its requirements, saying virtually. "We do not consider ourselves represented; therefore, we will not pay this tax. If you men govern this nation, then, for shame's sake, support your own government. We no more wish to pay our money for you to use as you please, to maintain an American government, which, by its own definition, is none of ours, any more than we have to pay Spain for her rule in Cuba; therefore, take your tribute in your own way."

They have taken it. "According to the laws themselves have made," and having their full "pound of flesh," why must they trouble themselves to scoff at the little womanly expression of pity for the dumb creature that owed all its well-being to its owners care? Why are they not content? Is it that they wish to pretend that not one agonizing drop was wrung from the tender hearts of women in the process of law? Is it past man's belief that woman may love and pity what she has reared and cared for? If so let him, scoff on.

South Glastonbury, Jan. 10.   R E. B.

From the Hartford Courant, Jan. 17th.

THE SMITH DEFENSE FUND.

LETTER FROM MRS. HOOKER.

Mrs Isabella B. Hooker of this city, has written the following letter to the Misses Smith of Glastonbury, whose letter about the seizure of their Alderneys by the tax collector we recently printed;—

To the Misses Smith of Glastonbury :—

Dear Friends :—In accordance with the

excellent suggestion of the Springfield *Republican* I send you five dollars for the Smith defense fund, only wishing it were five hundred instead. But I am hoping to emphasize your brave protest in another way. I have engaged Susan B. Anthony, who has rightly been called the John Hampden of America, to tell in our state, in as many towns as will consent to hear, the story of her being denied the right of trial by jury by a judge of the United States; and it can hardly be that when the just men of our little state shall learn how powerless they are, however willing, to protect women who have no power to protect themselves, they will not long continue to close the ballot boxes against us. A new Smithfield fire has been lighted it would seem, but thank God the flames will burn for illumination and not for destruction, and the day cannot be far distant when it will be seen that you who worked so faithfully for the emancipation and enfranchisement of the black man, and who now lead the van in the battle for woman's freedom are really apostles of that true christian liberty which knows neither Jew nor Greek, neither bond nor free, neither male nor female. It was well that your Alderneys were left you till after the 16th of December, that you might have their delicious cream in the *tea* you drank on that day in commemoration of our fathers energetic protest against taxation without representation. I am not sure that "kine couchant" on the grassy slope of the beautiful Connecticut should not be adopted as the emblem of our peaceful suffrage banner— but however that may be we surely are near the end of our warfare, and God grant that we may use our freedom wisely and well.

I am, with profound esteem, your fellow worker.   ISSABELLA B. HOOKER.

'Not a drop of that milk shall ever come into the house, for it seems just as if it were stolen,' said the heroic wife of the man whose shed had been the pound in which the town of Glastonbury put Miss Smith's cows, making her pay for the same. These words have in them the ring of that by which revolutions are carried. God bless the true hearted woman!

Woman's Journal.

RESOLUTIONS PASSED AT THE RHODE ISLAND WOMAN
SUFFRAGE ASSOCIATION,
PROVIDENCE, JANUARY 1874.

Resolved. That we heartily approve the noble stand for principle taken by Miss Abby Smith and her sister of Glastonbury, Conn., in refusing to pay taxes for the support of a government, which denies their representation without just cause.

Resolved. That we sympathize with them in the persecution which has followed their act, while at the same time we welcome them to the honorable company, whose praises have so recently been sung at "tea parties" all over the land—of those who dare offer assistance to tyranny, by *deeds* as well as *words*: and that we hope and believe their example will be followed by others, until our laggard legislators are scourged to their duty in regard to woman, by the whip of a public sentiment which tolerates no injustice.

            ANNA C. GARLIN,
            Cor. Sec. R. I. W. S. A

MRS. ELIZABETH CHACE. President.
MRS. LOUIS J. DOYLE. Char. Ex. Com.

From the Providence Press, Jan. 19th 1874.

ABBY SMITH'S COWS.

SELF GOVERNMENT OF WOMEN.

To the Editor of the Press :—

A friend has called my attention to an article in your paper entitled "The spirit of '73 Revived," which is, I must own, a most charming essay, and one that fairly illustrates the subject of woman's refusal to submit to taxation without representation, from a man's point of view; let me add, from a kind and good man's point of view. While you so accurately described the high position in life of those honorable ladies, did you not consider what an outrage it is upon humanity that such ladies should be denied the right of self government, while every man, by observing certain conditions, can vote to make the laws that women must obey.

The men of Glastonbury are not worse than other men; indeed, I think they are unequalled for benevolence of character, to speak of them generally; but the interest of the best of men are not identical with those of women. I cannot forbear to say here, that the revolution which brought freedom to the men of this land, brought nothing to American women but the honor of being governed and taxed by men of all colors, races and conditions, instead of the king and nobles of the mother country.

In characterizing the action of the Misses Smith as "foolish," did you reflect that women have presented numbers of petitions, praying the rulers of this land to grant them the privilege of self-government, that their prayers have been in vain, that even the promise given them by the party in power was a cheat, that a woman has been denied the right of trial by jury, (?) and that the condition of a class that submits to oppression grows even more intolerable? The first efforts of the men of America against the power of George the Third were as lawless, as weak and as ill-directed as are those of a woman who refuses to pay her taxes.

The saddest part of the whole matter is the utter inability of the men to assist the ladies in their struggles for the rights of self government. "The men of Glastonbury cannot," we are told, "consent to grant the wishes of the Misses Smith, without inaugurating a rebellion." Strange! Has democracy so hampered men that they cannot grant their fellow citizens, who' are only asking to share with them the highest privilege of humanity, at least their sympathy? Among all classes in England were found those who wished success to Americans in their struggle for freedom, and who aided them also. The triumvirs were not so bound that they could not remit the tax for a part of the suppliant women at Hortensia's pleading, and even Powhattan could break his laws when a woman implored him to be merciful. But the men of Glastonbury could not let the women vote at their town meetings, nor remit her tax, nor wait for her tribute a few months, with twelve per cent. interest upon it, promised and secured. Truly, partial freedom must enslave all.

The warning at the close of your article, which, it is to be hoped, will not be taken as a suggestion, gave me the knowledge of the sensation that a southern slave must have felt when threatened with the lash for learning to read.

Innocence and good intentions are not safe-guards against tyrants, still, I believe "naughty man" will think twice before he proceeds to such extreme measures; because, if he reflects, he will see that it may endanger man's happiness to have woman awake to a sense of her insecurity under man's laws and governments.

ROSELLA E. BUCKINGHAM.

So. Glastonbury, Jan. 13th.

From the Hartford Courant, Jan. 22, 1874.

LETTERS FROM THE PEOPLE.

THE GLASTONBURY MATTER AGAIN.

To the EDITOR *of the* COURANT :—

Whether the men of Glastonbury have the right to permit women to vote or not, it is evident that they think they have by their ingenious confession in THE COURANT that the town authorities voted upon the question last spring, and were unanimous against it.

Now if the first part of that assertion is correct, we were deceived, for we were told by the town officers that the registrars, by not allowing us to be properly registered, had taken all power to act in the case out of their hands; and, if the last part is true, we were deceived in that also, for we were personally assured by three of the four gentlemen before whom we pleaded our cause, that their votes would have been given in our favor. Consequently we had not the least doubt that the right we claimed would soon be granted to us, when suddenly the news that Miss Anthony had been denied the right to a trial by jury, came like a blight to all our hopes and made us certain that women had nothing to expect from man's benevolence or his promises, as far as her right to self-government is concerned. And our association enjoins it upon us all to show our earnestness in this matter by refusing to pay taxes, and guarantees that no woman shall suffer in " estate " by taking this course.

What the men of the town can do is to instruct their representatives to aid the women's cause when it is next brought before them in the legislature.

I wish it to be understood that I make no reflections upon the conduct of the men of Glastonbury, in the above. I do not believe that better, or more kind and considerate men exist, but the most upright man, among those he deems his political peers, does not consider it a great wrong to put off a woman's petition with fair, unmeaning words. The present party in power has set the example in its last Presidential campaign, and then, men are so much in the habit of deceiving themselves in regard to everything connected with women's suffrage that it is no wonder that it becomes a trivial matter to give a delusive answer to a woman.

SOUTH GLASTONBURY, Jan. 20th   R. E. B.

From the Hartford Daily Times, Jan. 22, 1874.

THE MISSES SMITH INTERVIEWED BY DR. C. C. DILLS, DENTIST OF HARTFORD

With spirits depressed, on account of American politics generally, and the sale of the Smith-Alderney-cows for taxes in particular, we started for Glastonbury, feeling, perhaps, here a

> " Lovely maid, with arms extended,
> Loudly for protection calls "—
> With which maid, if wed, defended
> Goes the *Alderney that bawls*—Cow-per.

Now, we are naturally gallant; we feel just as generous toward woman as man has ever shown himself by his laws, or as shown practically by the Massachusetts man who received $50,000 by his wife, and, dying within a year, willed it all back to her—provided she remained his widow. Perhaps our feelings in visiting the Misses Smith can be preambled and resolved thus :—

WHEREAS, We understand that two highly cultivated maiden ladies, bearing the objectional name of Smith, have three miles of good onion or tobacco land, *taxed without any possible representation ;* and

WHEREAS, That taxation without representation is adding serious trouble to evident loneliness; and

WHEREAS, We know how it is ourself to be lonely, even without the burden of estate ; now therefore

Resolved, We may be induced to relieve one of the said ladies of her name, and perhaps the other of her property—" constructively."

Thus we started out, a fair representative of our noble sex. But when, upon seeing the ladies, we were assured they had "managed to get along" past "the alloted time of life," and were bound to fight it out on this line, we thought, after all, how their recent experience with man must have made them hate his name more than they could their own; and so, remembering Punch's advice about marriage — "Don't!" — we didn't even mention this main object of our visit at all in the least.

Yet we were amply repaid for our call; were well received, invited to tea, hospitably entertained, and fully convinced, not only of our hostesses' "equality," but of our own positive inferiority.

The Misses Smith need no protection in any fair fight. Not all the "Selectmen" of Glastonbury, backed by the State and headed by Gen. Grant, could have got their pet cows from them, had they not resorted to a low, mean, cow-herdly manner of filching them.

When sifted of all irrelevant matter—such as this controversy may now well dispense with—the Misses Smith affair is but a fit centennial celebration of the Boston tea party—a perfect parallel, differing only in the parties making the demonstrations In each case law may have been disregarded, but the American government is based on the principle evolved — which principle does not, in itself, discriminate between sexes. No great principle has ever been enunciated, or fought or, by us that does not apply equally to every individual, and lead logically to woman—suffrage. So long as we deny this we but shirk the real issue, and show ourselves either inconsistent and morally weak, or physically strong and selfish—differing only in degree from pronounced barbarism.

It seems to us, by the steps already taken, we should realize how barbarous governments naturally are, and, thus distrusting ourselves, stride the more rapidly on towards even our ideals—feeling that, at best, "the remote future has in store forms of social life higher than any we can imagine, transcending the faith of the radical," or that "the doubtful precedents of one generation become the fundamental maxims of another." Not that we are dealing much with the ideal when we grant to woman every right we claim for ourselves as "inalienable"; we have only to be consistent with principles already adopted, trusting their practical working, at most, as something not so clearly seen. But with the question of absolute right, or truth, once settled, all questions of expediency may ever be safely trusted to the adjustment of practical life. Besides, it were more just, and better becoming American

people, that American women be granted rights of even doubtful expediency rather than any should suffer at our hands the particular wrong we so justify our fathers in opposing, or that the American republic should still falter in the application of its fundamental principles.

We repeat, the Misses Smith are but adding their popular name to the enfranchisement of women. The only thing peculiar about their case is, they arrive at the same point from practical experience, which others reach by theorizing. These ladies are purely practical. They seem neither to see, think or care, whether or not the town of Glastonbury can grant them the right to vote;—they simply know where the shoe pinches, and there they look to remedy. Miss Abby's theory is, if the town can't help them under the law, it elects the legislators who can change the law. Her course may, after all, be as practical as any. Certain it is, these sisters prove themselves good agitators, and we saw many letters addressed to them, from the most noted men of the country, with checks as high as $25 inclosed for the cause. (Let it not be supposed that these ladies will appropriate one cent of this fund accumulating, even to their own indemnity; on the contrary, they only await practical suggestions concerning the fund, to become contributors themselves.) Meanwhile they are as obstinate as General Grant ever was, or as President Grant ever can be, and mean to renew this agitation twice a year, so long as they may live, or their property may hold out, or the government may persist in its inconsistency.

In our heading we promise to gratify, somewhat, the usual public demand for private history of those it becomes interested in. We do so the more freely in this case, both because the history of this family is most creditable and interesting—and because of the sensible assurance given us that the surviving members of it are not affected by little things that annoy people generally.

We find the father and mother of five daughters to have been, Zephania Hollister Smith, and his wife, Hancy, who set a good example to the future generations of Smiths, by rendering their common name beautiful *by contrast*, — in naming their children thus:—Cyrinthia Secretia Smith; Lorillia Alliliroy Smith; Hancy Sephina Smith; Julia Avolina Smith; Abby Hadassa Smith. None of these sisters ever married; we did not ask if their names prevented; we did not ask if they had been asked to marry; —as before shown, we did not even ask if they wanted to marry—we did not want to be merely inquisitive, we only asked the simple (?)question : How comes it, that a family of such unquestionable attainments (as we shall show these ladies to have possessed) yet seemed to have so foiled God's evident designs concerning us in the matter of—well, say marriage? Echo but answered this question, as far as the answer we sought is concerned—but then, perhaps no one can answer such questions satisfactorily, the way things are going just now. We did not get an answer, though, and one somewhat significant in its general bearings upon our subject; it was this: that the father had imbibed a prejudice against marriage laws, and a distrust of man's chivalry, while discharging his duties as a lawyer! Ah—thought we; did that father, before 1850—when he died—discern evidences of "man's inhumanity to woman" that the law does not even yet admit? Though the father only exhibited his convictions in a mild and general way by withholding special opportunities for company, and always speaking as if the daughters would remain together, yet it must have had its effect, as no other special cause operated.

The father had been a Congregational minister, but becoming troubled with religious questionings he sought advice of the Rev. Mr. Wildman, of Southbury, who answered him: "I have thought just as you do, but I am too old to dig, and ashamed to beg; you are young. I advise you to quit the ministry." He did so at once, and afterward studied law with Judge Brace, and located at Glastonbury, where Mrs. Smith bought the present homestead.

There are many points of interest and peculiarity connected with the family, which we would be glad to mention, but space forbids. The mother is constantly alluded to as "a remarkable woman." She was a good French scholar, and, we believe, learned to read her Hebrew Bible after she was seventy years old. As a Biblical student, all her children patterned after her —the father always saying, "read your Bibles for yourselves." Miss Julia has written out the Bible, in translations, *five times*—twice from the Hebrew, twice from the Greek, and once from the Latin. Miss Abby is equally a theologian—most strikingly after the peculiar and original manner of Matthew Arnold's "Literature and Dogma." Disregarding every outside help, she confines herself strictly to the Bible, and finds prevading it *a spirit worthy of God*, and which elicits her sincere love and worship of Him. A most earnest defender of the Bible as from God, she yet says of miracles and Christ—in the very midst of religious enthusiasm, and with a simple innocence *simply indescribable*— "I really don't know whether miracles were

ever performed or not, I rather doubt that they were; I don't know what about Christ —I only know, or care, that I am freed from all forms of possible concern when I can go direct to God, which I do freely, in the deepest devotion." She constantly speaks of a "deep under-current" of the Bible, which is truth—but which language is too "perishable" to convey perfectly through all times alike. So her religion is too transcendental to express definitely, but she knows it exists, in a very practical, and the only practical manner for her. She does not care for a single literal interpretation; she only values language as conveying a faint idea of eternal truth. She would say with Arnold: "To understand that the language of the Bible is fluid, passing, and literary, not rigid, fixed, and scientific, is the first step towards a right understanding of the Bible." As a remarkable coincidence between the position attained by an unpretending private Biblical student on the one hand, and a noted one on the other, we can but speak of Matthew Arnold in connection with Abby Smith. Miss Abby protests she is not in accord with any known doctrine, while certainly Arnold is not. We can but suggest as well, that either the practical position of Miss Abby, or the theoretical one of Arnold, is worthy of consideration by those who may be tempted to give up the Bible altogether, because of their failure to give it any satisfactory literal interpretation.

We must not now neglect to mention, that one of these sisters was an artist of positive ability, as sufficiently proven by her paintings now at the homestead. And thus, more or less, each member of the family was educated with reference to, and practiced some specialty. The mother died some time after the father, and three of the sisters died at intervals of seven years each.

The love existing between the members of this family has been most intense; in fact, the surviving sisters unite in saying that they would rather be deprived of the ordinary ties of relationship than incur the risk of separation by death. Even the observed *attachment* for their cows becomes a serious rather than a jocular matter, when one knows all the circumstances.

c. c. d.

East Hartford, January 21st 1874.

From the Boston Post.

THE GLASTONBURY WAR.

Correspondence of the Boston Post.

GLASTONBURY, CONN., JAN. 21, 1874.

THE TOWN.

Within a time, comparatively brief, this

little town has risen from obscurity to be the centre of a public interest that has burst all local barriers and spread itself over all parts of the country where the political and civil rights and the destiny of women are discussed, and it suddenly finds itself famous through the spirited and determined position assumed by the Misses Smith, the practical champions of the old maxim with a new application, that "taxation without representation is tyranny."

Their house stands upon one of the commanding elevations, of which the place has seven fold more than old Rome, and looks modern, though that impression is conveyed by its fresh and well-kept exterior, for it is over a hundred and thirty years since its timbers were laid. Miss Abby Smith, whose quaint, vigorous and graphic descriptions of the two ceremonies, serving the legal attachment and auctioning off the Alderneys, have been given in full in your columns, answered the ring at the door and cordially inviting the writer in merely on the strength of a card, without waiting with chilling suspicion until any business could be explained. She is a lady upward of 70 years of age, judging from appearances, which I believe the sister's own statements confirm; rather above the medium height, with a face in which culture and kindness mingle to a marked degree. Her carriage is vigorous and her general manner though utterly devoid of haughtiness indicates that independance and firmness she has so fully demonstrated. She led the way, first into a large square room in which were a spacious and angular bay-window, where her plants were wont to be kept, and an old-fashioned fire-place, which showed that taste and comfort were both considered. This was the family sitting-room on most occasions, but she passed through it to a cosy little " snuggery" beyond, evidently used as a study where sat her sister, Miss Julia E., vigorously writing, very likely in regard to the matter which they have taken up with so much earnestness. Miss Julia is of slighter physique than her sister, but more rapid in her movements and a faster talker, though both talk well, and they could hardly hold more harmonious views did the same brain do the thinking for both. Consequently, it is not necessary to distinguish the speaker in a summary of their views, since both contributed freely to the rapid review of the situation. When assured that the stand they had taken was receiving notice and awakening interest in Boston, quite as much as in nearer places, they both remarked in a breath that it was wonderful and something that they little dreamed of when they took successive steps in their peculiar line of action. Perhaps the events that led these ladies to apply so persistently for suffrage were not of their own origination.

OPENING OF HOSTILITIES.

Early last Spring Mrs. Buckingham, and other talented women of Glastonbury who take the same stand as the Misses Smith in regard to suffrage, were voluntarily informed by one of the Registrars that their names could be registered, and when the Board met these three ladies, with two others, applied, and their names were set down in the form. The Registrars then promised to send word when the Selectmen would admit voters. Nothing was heard from them, however, and at this point the narrative of the Misses Smith became quite amusing, as they told how they followed up the secret sessions of these town authorities to compel a hearing, and at last cornered the Selectmen, to be told that the word "male" had not been expunged from the Constitution, and that they did not wish to do anything contrary to law. The Registrars denied the right of appeal also, and when the petitioners found from outside authority that they could appeal they were informed that it was too late, and they must wait another year. In March, however, they attended a town meeting and were received with extreme cordiality by almost all the members of a large gathering, and this evidence of good feeling and the favorable light in which the great majority seemed to regard their claims were highly gratifying and encouraging, and established to the entire satisfaction of the ladies the good influence that the female presence would exert upon town-meetings. In November several occasions were set when they might address the town authorities and vote upon what they considered the inequalities and injustice of the position in which they were placed, and the liberty to make their statements was respectfully granted and listened to in the same spirit, and no answer was made to it.

THE ALDERNEYS UNDER THE HAMMER.

The ladies claim that they were waiting for some action to be taken upon the proposition advanced when the cows were seized, and this seizure and sale, which they emphatically style an outrage, they attribute not to the sentiment of the town's poeple, but to the alleged vindictiveness of a single individual. It is only in connection with this affair that they so much as hint at a reproach of their neighbors for a lack of sympathy. When mingled with them to give expression to their views or "demands," as they term it, they had on all occasions been cordially greeted, but while this transaction was taking place at the auction-block forty men stood silent, all waiting," said Miss Abby, "to buy an Alderney cow cheap," and with that purpose controlling them, so low were the offers, that four of the cows had to be bid in to fill the town's demand. This sale, not only of their property but of their pets, was looked upon as an arbitrary proceeding, all the more for the reason that on two previous occasions the Collector had assured them that their tax could lie by returning twelve per cent. interest, which they consented to pay, and at the very time when their cows were being sold, there were more than $2000 of uncollected taxes, and no one seemed able to explain why this amount should be allowed to run and two defenceless women brought so rigorously up to the very letter of the law.

EPISTLES OF SYMPATHY.

Should the sympathy which this case has awakened have any more extensive manifestation than at present, they will need the services of an amanuensis, since almost every mail brings several letters of encouragement and good cheer. Among others which they exhibited was one in the bold, firm hand of Amos Lawrence, dated "Near Boston," telling the ladies to fight out the battle which they had begun, and support should not be wanting. He also gave figures tending to prove that the unjust discrimination against women of which they complained was confirmed in many towns of the country. Massachusetts having her fair share of them. A prominent lawyer of Columbia, S. C., had written them in the same vein, enclosing a check of $25 as a substantial token of the sincerity of his convictions. All these letters have to be acknowledged, or at least it is the desire of the recipients that they shall be, and that is quite a serious task for one or two persons with a multitude of other duties. Still, they are glad to receive these evidences of moral support from all sides, and in the somewhat curious position that they now find themselves placed, there is after all more sugar than wormwood. Concerning the defence fund they had little to say. That is a matter entirely distinct from their control or influence, though some one did suggest that they should head the list for a fund with a hundred dollars, but they stand ready to defend with their own means the position they have taken, though perhaps in a broader application of the principle for which they are contending they might consent to its use.

A LOOK AT THE BRINDLE-HEADS.

A visit to the Smith estate would have been incomplete without a sight of the famous Aldeneys, and a request to see them was most cheerfully granted. In a warm and roomy yard stood the redeemed eight, chewing the cud of sweet contentment, and if Alderneys indulge in retrospect, perhaps comparing their comfortable quarters with those of the time when they were confined in a tobacco shed, 15 by 12, with their brindle heads ungently clasped in galling stanchions. These Alderneys were in the main interesting, not because they would have specially adorned a Smithfield fair, but because they had been the pivotal centres of an idea's development, a principle's evolution, and perhaps were destined to become historic. For the rest, their confidence in humanity showed that they had received such treatment as they could not lose for a single day without grieving. Passing to the house again, the many objects of interest which the parlor afforded were shown. The walls were covered with paintings, the work of a departed sister, some in oil and some in water colors, representing local landscapes, sketches of flowers, historical subjects, etc., etc., while the objects of adornment of different character by the same hand were numerous and interesting. Everything seemed to speak a strong element of artistic and literary taste throughout the family, since it is a fact already mentioned that Miss Julia has made three translations of the Bible from as many dead languages, the Greek, Latin and Hebrew. All their accomplishments, however, are not difficult to account for, since the sisters modestly declare that their mother was a lady of even greater and more unusual acquirements than they, while their father so the traditions of the village say, was the squire of old Glastonbury and the most eminent man in town, who left to his five daughters the paternal acres, fine educations, and thorough business principles. Of the sincerity and honesty of these ladies in the stand they have taken there can be no doubt after talking with them, and they have acquired enough of their father's legal lore to believe confidently that their claims are founded in law as well as justice. Some have accused them of making the opposition they have for merely sensational purposes, or to make a stir, and they rightly aver that if such was their object they have succeeded beyond the warmest expectations of the most sanguine; but there is no doubt that their motives are far higher whatever may be the diversity of opinion regarding the acts which flow from them.

AT THE VILLAGE GROCERY.

Of course the men who have refused to satisfy the demands of these ladies have another story to tell and another view to take. Guided by the suggestion of a fellow-voyager through the Connecticut icebergs, who was familiar with the place, your correspondent sought out the village store, or one or the village stores, as a place likely to be productive of a variety of opinions. The Collector of Taxes and Chairman of the Board of Selectmen have been beyond call, living in a remote part of this town running six miles north and south by nine east and west, but the village store has been doubtless fairly representative. The proprietor evidently favored the ladies' side to a considerable extent, and though none seemed quite prepared to say that they justified a defiance, of the laws as they understood them; all were careful to put themselves in a friendly position to begin with by citing the charity of these sisters, and many stories were told of the suffering that their hands and purses had alleviated. They spoke of one woman, bed-ridden and almost blind, whom they had helped by as much as $500, and of others whose dire necessities they had satisfied by parting with portions of their own clothing on the spot, and they had been in fact the sisters of charity for the place, visiting the sick, feeding the hungry, and going about seeking for wretchedness to alleviate, not waiting for misery to come to them. It is admitted that they have given more in private charity than any other two persons, if not all the other citizens of the town.

THE TAX LEVY.

But to return to the question of taxation, there seems by the confessions of all to have been considerable looseness in the general levy for some time. The town and its officers profess to put in the taxable valuation at one-half its real valuation, but this standard, it would seem, in the majority of cases, is lost sight of, and one that is very unreliable substituted. Thus the real valuation of the town is put at near $6,000,000. while the general levy is not placed at over $12,000,000. In the village store discussion on this point it was asserted in the affirmative that the Misses Smith could not reasonably complain of the valuation of their property, for the homestead was put into the list at $4500, while they could at any time take $15,000 for the place, which included an excellent house and a farm three miles long and twenty-two rods and a half wide, divided into meadow, tillage, grazing and woodland in convenient proportions. Most of their other property, amounting to perhaps $5000, is in bonds, etc., not taxable here. The affirmative contended also that the Board of Relief was provided for the reduction of too heavy taxes, and that they had never applied to that body. The answer of the Misses Smith to that has already been given; still, no doubt, many will be inclined to think that

nothing should be taken for granted in such a case, and that every means which the law provides for redress should be tried before measures are resorted to, concerning the propriety of which there are so many conflicting views. Taking the valuation at the figures named, however, it was declared a high and unjust one by the negative side, which quoted homesteads worth eight thousand dollars put into the list at $1200, that any rate, high or low, the Collector should have garnered the outstanding $2000 for the town Treasury before driving to the auction post the favorite cows of the most charitable people in town. Another resident, met elsewhere, was more bitter than, any of the gentlemen of the village store debating society, and claimed that the Misses Smith, after anti-slavery days went by, in which they were prominent actors, had watched and waited for something to take their place, and for that reason the suffrage movement was a God-send to them and eagerly embraced. He said also that one of their letters was incorrect in stating that they paid the highest taxes in town since he and several other citizens had paid higher; yet he was careful to acknowledge the many acts of benevolence that had caused them to seem like ministering angels to a number who had no other human consolation.

THE MODERATOR'S CONFESSION.

Your correspondent was fortunate in making the acquaintance of Mr. J. W. Hubbard, a liberal and intelligent Democrat, and naturally a leader in town matters. He was the Moderator of the meeting which these ladies addressed, and confessed the pleasure which he felt in listening to them, saying at the same time that he should be happy to have them vote at the same polls as himself, provided they acquired the privilege in a way that should be consistent with the dignity and spirit of the laws, though he was disposed to look on this excitement as a "tempest in a teapot."

NOBODY HURT.

Whatever may be the result of this contest, which will, perhaps, have a wider field than Glastonbury, there is no one hurt as yet, not even the cows. The ladies, who hold a central place, have been proven by those opposed to them in opinion examples of unpretentious benevolence, which would make the world better if there was more of it, and so far as can be judged from conversation and observation, they were never held in higher esteem and respect by the citizens of Glastonbury than they are to-day, whether their destiny be success or failure.　　　　　　　　　F.

THE GLASTONBURY WAR.

Correspondence of the Boston Post.

GLASTONBURY, JAN. 22, 1874.

A PLEASANT HOME.

It would be impossible for a purely disinterested person to remain long in the society of the Misses Smith and not be impressed with their earnestness and enthusiasm, as well as their courage, kindness and culture, for whether the world approves or disapproves of the position that they have taken all must admit that it requires no little self-assertion, independence and positiveness of character, to stand almost alone and combat the opinions that are grounded in the customs of ages. The spontaneous expressions of sympathy which they are constantly receiving, some of them over the signatures of men and women whose names occupy a high place in the lists of those remarkable for benevolence, public spirit and liberal ideas, are not in the least to be wondered at, and the number of them would be increased did all who sympathize with the movement understand the exalted characters and beautiful lives of these venerable and now famous ladies. The little "snuggery" or study, before referred to, into which Miss Abby ushered the POST correspondent, is just such a cosy corner as any literary person would like to occupy. It is a little room of less dimensions apparently than the tobacco shed in which the Alderneys were placed under temporary duress. Like the remaining rooms in the house it is neat, but it lacks the scrupulous orderly arrangement which they present. It is an attractive disorder, however, and with its piles of papers, its writing table and implements, with books convenient, it shows the purpose for which it has been set apart, and probably few passing travellers dream that in this modest farm-house has dwelt for half a century, in the full maturity of unusual talents, a family whose tastes, culture and refinement made their society worth the cultivation of the most famous men and women; but it is none the less to their credit that they continued content to occupy a narrower sphere than the one which they could have adorned. As Miss Abby opened the door which revealed the interior of this pleasant room, with its easy chairs and windows disposed east, south and west, as if to catch the first, the warmest and last rays of the sun, Miss Julia sat so deeply engrossed with her writing that she did not notice the advent of a stranger. Her writing-table was arranged more with a view to convenience and comfort than elegance, and she was so seated that when she wished to rest her mind she could gaze through the window directly in front upon

her brindle and red Alderneys placidly ruminating in the neat little yard beyond. Upon the announcement of a new comer, however, she dropped her work at once, snook hands with the utmost cordiality, and, leaving all abstractions, became in an instant an interesting companion. Her age is probable not far from that of her sister, and time has perhaps ploughed deeper furrows in her cheeks, but her eye is bright and kindly, and her manner is as sprightly as that of a young lady just out of her teens, and much more natural. The sister did not force a doleful tale of their grievances upon the POST correspondent, but spoke unreservedly upon invitation concerning that matter, and were quite as ready to speak of other topics when they were broached, and the two or three hours' interview might have been extended with pleasure to the initiator if time had permitted. During the stay Mrs. Kellogg, the lady referred to as Mrs. K. in the various communications which Miss Abby sent to the Springfield Republican concerning the sale of their cows, dropped in and was introduced to the correspondent. As she has been an active sympathizer with the ladies, and was a member of the protesting party during the auction sale, she deserves a place in this general description. She is a lady apparently not far from forty, with an intelligent, interesting face, and one that indicates the good judgment of these ladies in the selection of a prime minister, and Miss Julia said that she knew as much and felt as deeply concerning this whole matter as either she or her sister. She and her husband have the management of the place and the care of the stock, and the excellent understanding that exists between all parties speaks well for the fairness and honorable dealing of both sides. Mr. and Mrs. Kellogg will without doubt receive the meed of true fidelity when the Glastonbury struggle passes into history.

THE INTERVIEW.

Being at a loss at first to distinguish the two sisters the POST correspondent confessed his dilemma and asked for enlightenment.

MISS JULIA—Oh, this is Abby, (pointing to her sister, with a laugh), and she has had to bear the brunt of all the newspaper comments upon "Abby Smith's cows," while I have been allowed to stay in the background.

MISS ABBY—But Julia has just as much to do with this movement as I have, only I happened to write the letters which opened the controversy, and since then I have had the bulk of proprietorship in this whole affair; still I dont mind; we want this principle for which we are contending kept before the people, and perhaps that will be done as well by the remarks of those opposed to us as by those in our favor.

CORRESPONDENT—The vigor and directness of your contributions to the Springfield Republican gave you a literary reputation, to which perhaps may be attributed some of the wide interest that you have awakened.

MISS ABBY—Well, I am sure that I made no attempt after effects in these communications. I had a plain story to tell, and I wished to tell it in a way that should include all the facts in readable and comprehensive form.

CORRESPONDENT—Will you tell me how this movement was commenced, and what plans you have formed in relation to it for the future?

MISS JULIA—We have no definite plan of future action any more than we have reached this point by the development of any organized policy. We have taken the steps thus far that seemed right, considering the injustice which we had to endure, and our course in the future will depend upon that of those with whom we have to deal. We have been told that the valuation of our property was no more oppressive than that of others in town, and that is true; but these others are women, also. When a man asks that his assessment shall be reduced, the authorities do not refuse. It would not do to offend a voter.

CORRESPONDENT — The attachment of your cows by the Collector was entirely unexpected to you?

MISS JULIA—We had no reason to expect any such outrage, for we had been visited twice before by that officer, and each time, instead of hinting at or threatening any such arbitrary process, he said that our taxes could lie as well as not by the payment of twelve per cent., at least until the town had fully considered our demands and given us some answer. At the town meetings at which we applied for a hearing we were put off twice, the reason advanced being a press of other business. At last we were allowed to speak and the meeting heard us through to the end, quietly and respectfully, but no one replied when we had concluded. It was after this, a few days, that the Collector made his third call to see about our taxes. We told him that we had heard nothing concerning any action taken upon our petition, and that we were waiting until that had been considered before doing anything. Yet that seemed to make no difference with him, and the cows were attached.

MISS ABBY—But this was not the work of the townspeople, our neighbors. They would never have performed such an act so promptly. It all originated with Mr. ——, and I told the Collector that it was this

man's doings and he did not deny it.

CORRESPONDENT—Was any reason assigned for refusing the 12 per cent. which you offered to pay while the question of your taxes was pending?

MISS JULIA—None whatever, and I cannot see what objection could have existed since there are two thousand dollars outstanding now on these same conditions, and no movement is made to collect it by attachment and sale: but that is on the property of voters, which makes the protection of suffrage seem all the more desirable to us. It would have been perfectly safe to let this money lie. The town did lose something a few years ago by the bankruptcy of a manufacturing company for whose taxes they were waiting, but we, while not wishing to hoard up anything, spend no more than our income, and are in no immediate danger of failing, as I told the Collector.

THE ALDERNEYS AGAIN.

At this point the visit was made to the Alderney cattle in the little yard already referred to. The stock in sight included eight, one of which had been spared the ignominy of the auctioneer's hammer in accordance with that boasted liberal statute that spares the poor man his last cow. These animals ranged in age all the way from the amiable and maternal old brindlesides through several generations until the yearling, the baby of the happy family, was reached. There was some variety of color, but the brown crock upon a red background was the predominating mark of this interesting group. Cows, like dogs and horses, are influenced to a remarkable degree by human training and associations, and the Alderneys seemed to say in their quiet happiness that they had enjoyed unusual advantages in that particular. Reared in freedom, their previously untrammelled lives felt the restrictions of that tobacco shed as much as a Western hunter would if forced into a dungeon, and perhaps they made for one night at least the loudest protest that had been heard against that peculiar way of paying taxes. There seemed to be such a good understanding between the cattle and their mistresses that the correspondent inquired if it was not the hardest trial of all when they were driven resistingly away from their home.

MISS JULIA—I felt wretchedly, and could hardly sleep while the poor things were confined in that pent up place. They are all stock in raising which I have had a direct share, and their distress sorely tried me.

MISS ABBY—We went down early to the auction sale, and hardly expected the coolness with which we were received, but the bidding explained it. There were forty men standing around, intent on buying an Alderney cow cheap, and we had to bid in four of the best ones to satisfy the demand, and a happy lot they were when they found themselves home once more.

After some conversation on miscellaneous matters the Post correspondent took his departure, declining with regret the cordial offers of hospitality which the ladies extended.

WHAT THEY EXPECT.

Doubtless the friends of woman suffrage will be pleased and encouraged to be assured that these ladies are not putting themselves forward in this movement merely to embarrass the town authorities. They are taking this course because they confidently expect to succeed; indeed, they look upon it as a certainty, and Miss Abby, when interrogated on that point, replied with emphasis. "Of course it's right, and it MUST succeed when people come to look upon all sides of it. Why shouldn't we be allowed to vote and say what shall be done with our property as well as the man to whom we extend charity and who counts one at the polls, whether or not he knows anything or is worth anything?" The first reason, that their cause must succeed because "it is right," may seem to some a "woman's argument," though eminent theologians use it as well. The next reason is a strong one and harder to answer. It would be hardly fair to say that these ladies had a hobby, for they would not have waited until this time of life before developing it. Besides, it is not those who have the business of a large farm to look after, literary and artistic work to do, and act the good Samaritans for a community that run into hobbies. Moreover, this is not a good town in which to nurse a theory merely for the sake of something to talk about. They have evidently made up their minds to test legal and Constitutional objections to the utmost, or rather, by acting according to their own views of what is lawful as well as just; force the town to prove what it claims or else yield what they demand as their due. The end is not yet, and the pastoral politics of Glastonbury will doubtless continue to attract attention for some time to come. **F.**

From the Springfield Republican, Jan. 30, 1874.

THE SMITH SISTERS.

To the Editor of the Republican :—

GLASTONBURY, CT., Friday, January 23.

It is hardly a fortnight, I believe, since you requested "reinforcements" to be

poured in to our aid, but I can wait no longer to tell you they have "come at your call" from all parts of the land. We have not only sympathy but every assurance of assistance and support, and they all seem to come from the most highly educated part of the community. The mail, every night, brings in a bundle of papers and letters that seems wonderful to us. Last night brought us a check of $100, and among the rest an anonymous card, postmarked Newport, R. I., in a man's hand, which I will copy to show you the spirit of all these communications: "Take good care of the cows, Abby. Fight on, we will break down the obstacles and prepare the way for those that come after us through God. Amen." Among the numerous letters we have received is one from Amos Lawrence, telling us to fight it out and we shall not lack support, and another from a lawyer in Columbia, S. C., inclosing a check for $25.

ABBY H. SMITH AND SISTER.

RESOLUTIONS PASSED AT THE MASSACHUSETTS WOMAN SUFFRAGE ASSO. JAN. 1874.

3. *Resolved*, That the recent seizure and public sale of the property of the Misses Smith, of Glastonbury, Ct., for the payment of taxes, in the assessment of which they were denied a voice, is a repetition of the crime of the British government, in its attempt to enforce upon our revolutionary ancestors the odious Stamp Act and Tea-tax; but with the added meanness in this case, that, not only is the crime committed by fathers, husbands and sons against their own mothers, wives and daughters, but also in flagrant violation of their own avowed political principles.

4. *Resolved*, That having carefully considered the matter in the light both of moral principle and political expediency, we heartily approve the course of these heroic women, in their peaceful resistance to the demands of arbitrary power, and we cordially commend their example to all who are able and willing to make the requisite personal sacrifice, believing as we do that no other issue can be raised with the present despotic government of the country which will so surely accomplish its speedy reformation.

From the Nantucket Enquirer and Mirror, Jan. 31, 1874.

A TOAST GIVEN AT THE HOUSE OF MISS MARY EASTMAN.

To the Selectmen of Glastonbury : The first gun fired on Fort Sumpter, rang the death-knell of negro slavery in the Southern States. The persecution of the Misses Smith by the Selectmen of Glastonbury, decides the question of Woman Suffrage in America.

EQUAL RIGHTS FOR ALL.

Our cause is gaining every day,
We're sure of its success,
For with our friends we count the first,
From pulpit, school and press.

From the Hartford Times, February, 2, 1874.

TO THE EDITOR OF THE TIMES.—Does might make right? It is something certainly to have the benefit of a government, no matter what kind of a goverment it may be. King George would have told his colonists that they were entitled to his protection, and he was entitled to be paid for it. He might also have said that the famous Tea Party of 1778 was an attack upon irresponsible persons, and a destruction of private property, to show a disrespect to public measures. "You should have applied to me," he would have said, and if he had been answered, "We have, and have been denied the right we claimed," he would probably have advised him to be content with that denial. But he was a King; and did not govern by the light of the Declaration of Independence.

I am glad that you have told us where to apply for permission to vote, because you seem to believe that the power rests with the Legislature to grant our wishes. Now it only remains to be seen to which power the representatives will refer us, the general government or the constituents. If the men of the towns desire to give women the right to vote, they can do so, for the power rests with the people and not with their servants. The truth is that women are subjected to an intolerable tyranny, and by a government that pretends to derive its just powers from the consent of the governed.

To have seen King George and his nobles assembled in Parliament to make laws for all the people must have been a soul-inspiring spectacle; but when our rulers meet at the polls, we are told that the sight is an unfit one for a woman to look upon.

I do not see that woman has gained anything for the help she gave to man in the American Revolution. We are human beings and therefore entitled to the benefit that the Declaration of Independence gives to all humanity; and it is a shame to men that they can answer our appeals to them for the right of self-government with the contemptuous grin of a sham superiority, or with solemn mockery.

Women have petitioned both the high and the low for a share in their own government, and, at last, they have taken a way to show themselves in earnest. Two of the noblest, and kindest-hearted and the most law-abiding ladies that I have ever known —ladies who, for their charities alone, are an honor to their native town—have refused to be taxed without representation, and men of education and refinement, who know well that their only safeguard in this country's government is the power of the ballot, can find nothing better to say about the case than to suggest what "may be equitable" as far as "spinsters" are concerned, and to take the trouble to point women to all the laws that men have enacted for their own benefit. King George could have done no less.

Jonathan has chasseed long enough alone to the tune of Yankee Doodle, and the time has now arrived for Jemima to "figure in." She should be welcomed to an enlarged sphere of action, for the help of pure women is needed at this very time to guard against the dangers that inevitably spring from such a false system of government as ours. False in this, that while professing to be a democracy, it is a detestable despotism of men.

You say that "it may be that equity demands that spinsters should be placed in the same category with negroes before the passage of the fifteenth amendment." What a concession! What if equity should demand that bachelors should be placed in that category? In speaking of these women who have failed to provide themselves with husbands," you do not tell us how that provision should have been made. Marriage is the sweetest and holiest relation in life—see "young love's dream," and all that sort of thing—and I protest it is too bad for you, who may, for all that I know, be keeping one fair woman out of that state, and fifty others in a state of expectancy, to allude to the painful truth that old maids are to be pitied because they have not secured husbands, and thereby obtained a voice in the government. How they, by bestowing on some man a life interest in their property, could have gained anything so desirable, is the question, when it has been shown by man's law that it only costs a husband two thousand dollars to lodge a pistol ball at the base of his wife's tongue, thus depriving her of all voice forever. [I have since learned that it does not cost a cent; they will probably offer a small premium for such meritorious acts, before long.]

R.E.B.

From Harper's Weekly, Feb. 7, 1874.

SAM ADAMS AND MISS ABBY H. SMITH.

Mr. Robert C. Winthrop and Mr. Josiah Quincy, two of the most eminent citizens of Boston, eloquently extolled at the Centennial meeting in Faneuil Hall the men of a hundred years ago, who threw the tea overboard, and led the American Revolution to the cry, "Taxation without representation is tyranny." They justly praised Sam Adams, and we all cry Amen. We invite the attention of the distinguished gentlemen to Sam Adams *redivivus*—Sam Adams in the person of Miss Abby H. Smith, of Glastonbury, Connecticut. Miss Smith and her sister own a farm in that town. They are honest, industrious, useful citizens, but they have been oppressed exactly as Sam Adams was. King George and his ministers and his redcoats have also re-appeared in Glastonbury in the form of the town meeting and the town constable. Miss Smith, like Sam Adams has protested. She has appeared before the town meeting, and stated that the owners of part of the property in the town tax the owners of the other part without consulting them, and enforce their will. It is not denied, she said, that she and her sister manage their property as well as their neighbors so far as the laws permit. Is it more just or right, she asks, to take a woman's property without her consent than a man's without his consent? Taxation without representation is tyranny, exclaims Miss Smith. Sam Adams says Amen. What do the eloquent Mr. Winthrop and Mr. Quincy say? King George is as contemptuous at Glastonbury as he used to be at Windsor and at St. James's. On the 1st of January he sent General Gage, in the form of the collector, to sell Miss Smith's property to pay the taxes which had been laid upon it without any voice having been allowed to her. She asked that he would begin by selling the part of the farm that was farthest from the house. General Gage replied that he must first take personal property, according to law. He therefore took seven of the eight Alderney cows belonging to Miss Smith and her sister. They pleaded hard for a respite until they could petition to be allowed to own their land as the men owned theirs. Nor was a delay unprecedented, for the town had waited for its taxes from a factory company for several years There was no risk in waiting, but the collector would not listen. "There are $2000 due the town for taxes," said Miss Smith, "from voters, who are released by paying twelve per cent. interest. Give us the same indulgence." But the collector answered by taking seven Alderney cows, and on the eighth day afterward the best four of them were sold below their value to pay the tax and expenses. Miss Smith ends her letter, in which these facts are stated, by saying, "As the town now manage our property, we must soon be forced to the poor-house, and none are better acquainted with its inmates."

This story has excited much attention in New England. The Boston *Advertiser* reminds the authorities of Glastonbury that their conduct will be carefully watched. The Providence *Journal* advises every paper that comments upon the subject to send a marked copy to the officers of the town. And the Springfield *Republican* says that such a protest is worte a great many conventions and documents. The common reply will be, Let the foolish women pay their taxes, and then they can milk their own cows in peace. Dr. Sam Johnson said the same thing to Sam Adams, in a little pamphlet called *Taxation no Tyranny.* But Sam Adams was not converted, and the colonies were not converted, and Mr. Winthrop and Mr. Quincy and the rest of us applaud them for resisting the collector, and

undertaking a long and doubtful and wasting war rather than submit to pay taxes upon their property which they had had no voice in levying. But if Sam Adams and George Washington would not submit to this kind of taxation a hundred years ago, why should Miss Abby Smith and her sister submit now? If it was tyranny then, is it less tyranny now? If the Misses Smith are competent to own property in fee, and to manage it at their pleasure, can they be logically considered incompetent to express an opinion upon the taxes which may be laid upon it? Does taxation without representation cease to be tyranny, and become justice, when the taxed property-owner is a woman? This is the question to which a good-natured laugh at Miss Anthony does not seem to be an entirely satisfactory answer.

From the Hartford Times, Feb. 19, 1874.

The following verses were sent to the Misses Smith by some anonymous correspondent in Boston. The title of the piece alludes to the boy and drums called into service when the cows were sold.

THE DRUM OF GLASTONBURY.

The brave boys of Connecticut
  Went marching to the fight;
Beating their drums they onward strode
  To battle day and night.

They fought to keep this nation free;
  "The Union" was their cry;
Our fathers won us liberty
  And shall our country die?

What proud procession passes on?
  Why sounds the drum to-day?
Why to the sign-post through the town,
  Do people take their way?

Who answers to the roll-call now?
  Those seven cows, you see,
And forty men who rush to buy
  These cows—for liberty.

The drum that beat ten years ago
  To rebels—Right is Might,
Now wakens echoes round our homes
  That answer—Might is Right.

We choose to tax Miss Abby Smith
  To say she shall not vote;
The cows we now put up for sale
  Our liberties denote.

Oh! brave boys of Connecticut,
  Beat loud your battle drum;
To auction-block of liberty
  Bid all your men now come.

EXTRACT FROM A LETTER FROM WM. LLOYD GARRISON, TO MRS. FOSTER AT WORCESTER CONVENTION. FEBRUARY, 1874.

I see it is announced that among those expected at the meeting are those noble women, the Misses Smith of Glastonbury, Conn. The calm, dignified, uncompromising manner in which they have passed through a similar ordeal entitles them to the warmest sympathy and the highest commendation. The men of Connecticut who can persistently disregard their righteous protest are not worthy to touch the hem of their garments. With all my heart I thank them for what they have done with such admirable judgment and good sense. Let such examples be multip'led, and it will not be long before the injustice complained of will be remedied, and either there will be no disfranchisement on account of sex, or no taxation where there is no representation.

Yours has been a life of self-sacrifice in behalf of the downtrodden and oppressed. I offer you my heart-felt thanks and best wishes.

Yours in every conflict for the right,

WILLIAM LLOYD GARRISON.

NEWPORT, R. I., Feb. 15, 1874.

30

A SPEECH.

From the Boston Journal, Feb. 20, 1874.

MISS JULIA SMITH OF GLASTONBURY, CONNECTICUT, Was introduced and spoke substantially as follows: I want to say a few words, though I never spoke but once before in a public assembly in my life, and that a word or two in the noted town meeting. It is not probable I shall talk to the purpose, but I hope I shall be excused as I am only Abby Smith's sister. I always tried to make something of her, being older than she is, but she is so retiring that I cou d make nothing of her. None can be more astonished, and I may say gratified, than I am to find that her name all at once has come into such notoriety, and that we have been invited to address such an assembly of men and women as this. But I do think Abby Smith is somewhat indebted to her sister for her rising fame, for had I not raised those renowned Alderneys I am sure she would have missed half of her celebrity. Mrs. Hooker said the other day in her address at Willimantic, Conn., that Abby Smith and her cows were marching on like John Brown's soul. True enough they are marching on in the newspapers, through the length and breadth of the land, from Maine to California, and I thought last Saturday night that they might have crossed the Atlantic, for we received a London paper addressed to Miss Abby H. Smith from its editor favoring women's rights, but not a word about the cows. Mrs. Hooker has first rate talents for speaking, but I am only a matter of fact body and just state things as they happen. My sister and I are more astonished than any one else that those pet animals should be seized, as there was not the least necessity for it, as the tax was perfectly safe according to law, and that they should take them from women of our years, life-long inhabitants of our native place, always paying taxes, without making trouble and treating the town authorities with kindness and respect, and behaving generally as good citizens should do. No matter if men's taxes to the amount of $2000 lie till they are ready to pay, it would not do to let women have their way. They must pay when the men say, and they have no right to withold or to speak in the matter. They have the privilege of living on their homestead, own land, can bring up calves, though they cannot raise tobacco if they would. and they can walk or ride along the streets, and ought they not to pay one or two hundred dollars a year for such advantages as these? It is none of their business if we do claim taxes and apply the money to our own emolument without their consent. But how can we help it? We must obey the laws. No man, of course, is to blame, for though he can injure helpless women according to law as much as he

pleases, he has no power to redress the wrong. I did not come away off here in the depth of winter to talk against my own townsmen, for they are as good as other towns' people, had they not held my pet cows in durance vile seven days, though I do not believe many other towns would have driven off my pet calves; but let that go, for I do bel ve a great majority of them would let *us* vote, nor are they afraid of Judge Hunt or the laws, though they plead that now, but they did not last spring, when we were registered. The difficulty is it will let in all the Catholic women and other good for nothing working women. We say, "do right and let the heavens fall," leave the consequences with God. But no! and so they are all propping up the heavens with all their might. If we dispose of our stock so that in March they can find no outdoor personal estate, they can enter our house and lay hold of our ancient furniture, paintings and ornamental work of a deceased sister, which we value. But such personal estate must be moved twenty-one days before the sale at the auction block, and we shall have time to advertise our friends so that there may be an assembly that will show more sympathy and feeling for us than was manifested at the last auction sale. If any our friends in this assembly, and I think we have many here, should intend to visit us I hope they will come soon while we can entertain them in good style, for no dwelling is very comfortable without furniture. I think it will not be sold before April, We shall plead hard to keep it till warm weather, but I fear we shall receive no mercy at their hands, and must rest content that they can't shut us up as they did our cows, and what is worse still they cannot shut our mouths.

Miss Abby Smith made a few remarks and was greeted with applause. She said that their property would be offered for sale again in March, and she and her sister came to Worcester to learn some of the particulars of the cases arising here. She said that when she asked why they were treated as they had been, the only answer they received was that the law obliged them to do so. They had received letters of endorcement and pecuniary assistance from everywhere, at the rate of twenty-four per week. The matter seemed to them morally wrong. that men should have the power to take their money without some voice in the matter. If one part of the community can plunder another there is an end of harmony and civil government. Upon the subject of woman suffrage she would say, let those who know most, regardless of sex, take charge of affairs, and the question of sphere would take care of itself.

GLASTONBURY, CT., *Feb.* 7, 1874.

Dear Friend,—Among all the communications sent us from all parts of the country, none could be more agreeable to our feelings than the one received this evening from Philadelphia. You inquire of our affairs, as if by telling them we would be doing you a favor, when the favor is on our side. Our situation it is true, is a very peculiar one. The town of Glastonbury (of about 3000 inhabitants) in which we were born and have always lived, is seven miles south of Hartford, on the east side of the Connecticut. Its main street is six miles long, and is built half a mile from the river. Our house is a mile from the upper post-office, and two miles from the lower one, and half a mile from the town hall. The land on which it stands—the great cause of contention—extends three miles from the river east, and twenty-two and a half rods wide, mostly woods. We two only are left of one of its most ancient families—the best known of any in the place—standing alone with all the men of the town arrayed against us — for these men having always taken our money from us whenever they chose, seem determined, with one consent, to defend their power. Last fall we thought them great friends, and we decided to attend the town meeting and to lay our case before them. Though neither of us had ever spoken in public we thought if we did, they must see their injustice. This meeting was held Nov. 5. They treated us with much respect, and applauded us when we finished, but none answered a word. I will send you that speech and our interview with the collector afterward, contained in the *Woman's Journal* copied from the *Hartford Courant.* The collector had told us we might let our tax go on at 12 per cent., and we were wholly taken by surprise when he called New Year's day, and drove off our cows, of which we had not the least intimation. The tax then was only $101, and he took seven Alderneys leaving one—the poor man's portion. We begged him to leave another, but he would not, alleging that cows were cheap, and the other cried all the time they were gone. Had we not been at the auction block ourselves, the whole seven would, no doubt, have been sacrificed. Our tenant bid off four at a low price, which more than satisfied the tax and accruing expense, and the cows are now in our yard. There will be another tax claimed in March, and it is already threatened in a Hartford newspaper that the Alderneys will be taken again, but we mean to dispose of them. If they find nothing out of doors, we suppose they will enter the house and take our furniture; but that we can bear, for there will be no animal suffering in the case.

The defence fund was proposed by the *Springfield Republican,* to indemnify us for extra charges. It was entirely unlooked for by us, for we think we have property enough to support us while we live, neither do we wish to burden our friends. It has, however, much alleviated our feelings in finding we have true friends, and it also serves to astonish our adversaries, who see we are to suffer no loss by their actions. We have received communications of the most encouraging and sympathetic kind, from Maine to California, and even to Oregon. The men show the spirit of '76, telling us to fight it out to the bitter end, and not budge an inch, and we shall not want for support. We have reason to think public opinion will outweigh the law. Please give our thanks to the Radical Club for their spirited Resolutions, and accept of much love from

J. AND A. SMITH.

CITIZEN'S SUFFRAGE ASSO. PHILADELPHIA.

From the Springfield Republican.

ABBY SMITH AGAIN.

From Our Special Correspondent.

GLASTONBURY, CT., Monday, April 6, 1874.

This quiet old farming town has had another sensation, to-day, to gratify the local gossips and herald forth again its reputation over the land. About 10 o'clock a carriage drove up to the town-house, where the (male) "soverigns" to the number of a hundred or more were assembled to "exercise the highest right known to a freeman," chew tobacco and compare notes as to the weather and the prospect for the crops. From this carriage presently alighted the now famous "Smith sisters," and, Abby in advance, entered the town-house—a building quite after the conventional style for such an institution in old fashioned Connecticut towns, cheerless and unkempt. Curiosity was at once on the qui vive, and the idlers who had been sunning outside pressed in "to see the fun." Sitting down on a settee at the side of the room, the sisters entered into conversation with a townsman who has always treated them courteously, and informed him of their object in coming, which was to make one more appeal to male Glastonbury for justice. Meanwhile the expectant audience were speculating and commenting on the unexpected visitors, and, as one moved about the room, he might hear such comments as, "Well I wonder what's the trouble now?" "I don't like to see women unsex themselves," etc.,—the drift being plainly strong against the women. Finally the unexpected (and unwelcome) visitors approached the moderator's desk, and asked permission to address their fellow-townsmen. But the moderator was not at all anxious for any remarks from that quarter, and informing the women that the meeting was simply an electors' meeting, for which the polls must be kept open and unobstructed all the while, declared that no speaking could be legally allowed—a decision that was doubtless correct, technically, though there is little doubt that, if any prominent citizen had asked permission to say a few words for himself, it would have been granted him. There was no help for it, however, and so Abby and Julia withdrew, remarking rather pointed y on the injustice which refused them a hearing in the hall for which they had paid more than any voter in town.

Out-doors, in the women's train, followed the crowd, and, the love of fair play at last conquering prejudice, there were soon cries that the women ought to have a chance to speak, and presently suggestions that they could address the crowd out-doors almost as well as in the hall. The intrepid sisters were not slow to accept such an invitation, and there soon ensued one of the most unique spectacles in Connecticut annals. Mounting an old wagon which stood on the south side of the town-house, Abby Smith drew from her pocket the speech she had prepared, and read it to the assembled audience standing in front and on either side. Speaker, hearers and circumstances combined to make the scene a noteworthy one. In the wagon stood one of the two richest women in the town,—who between them are assessed a larger tax than any man in Glastonbury,—asking for an equal voice with her male fellow-tax payers; about her were gathered the voters who lay this tax,—a fair representation of the men who elect our governors and legislatures,—solid farmers, stalwart laborers, shiftless idlers, young men glad of anything out of the stereotyped order. Not a sympathetic audience, certainly; rather too much inclined to the boisterous merriment which the freedom of country life fosters; yet, on the whole, respectful, and not a little impressed before the speaker had reached the end.

ABBY SMITH'S APPEAL TO HER TOWNSMEN.

We come before you, gentlemen, in no spirit of defiance, but as fellow-citizens with you of the same place, having the interests with yourselves and the same love for the prosperity of the town. We wanted to see you and to reason with you, desiring that the difficulty which has arisen between us might be settled among ourselves, as brethren and sisters of the same family, to the satisfaction of both. We shall agree that towns should be regulated as families are regulated, that a natural feeling of affinity may exist among all that compose the household. If we are all of one family, would it not be well to look to our own individual families, to see how its members are dealt by? The first thing you will observe among them is, that each claims his or her own things, with which the other is not allowed to meddle. Unless this right is accorded to every one, there will be no peace among them, there will be no living together. The first thing a child says is "It is mine!" and will scream and fight to have it taken away from him by violence, though he will give it up by persuasion. There is no difference between boys and girls in this respect; the girls will yield their things no sooner than the boys. There is the same mind in both, for, being born of the same parents. they must have the same mind,—like produces like throughout the world. It is the mind we value. One is as necessary to the welfare of the whole family as the other; their advice and counsel must both be sought, for both are equally interested. What do we say of those young men that forsake the society of their sisters, and counsel together without them? We all know their way leads to ruin. But what should we say if the brothers should by agreement, without consulting their sisters, take their sisters property from them whenever they chose, and as much as they chose, alleging as an excuse, they had made a law among themselves they would do it. Are their sisters bound by such a law? Are we bound by such a law? The case is precisely the same. You all know it is not just. It is not doing as you would be done by, and as you are done by. We are perfectly willing to share the expenses of this large family equally with you, but as unwilling as you are, to be ruled over and have our property taken from us by force.

We have had sad experience of this power that rules over us to take whatever we own from us, and as much as it chooses to take. We have had-sad experience of being under no law but the irresponsible will of the men of the town, whose interest it is to take our property.. We thought they would allow us to own our cows, that we had raised with our own hands. But they tied up those young unimals seven days and seven nights in a close place, seven of them,—having never been tied before,—without hay or water, near by, and whether they were supplied with either could not be known by those that put them there, living several miles off, and at last driven to the sign-post to be sold to the highest bidder. All this was more trying to our feelings than any act that was ever done to us. And to whom was it done? To two lone women, standing by themselves,—the last of their family, among the town's oldest inhabitants, having no relatives to take their part, and none to stand up for them. And by whom was it done? By their natural protectors (they having had no brothers), into whose hands they were paying more in money, as appears by the collector's books, than any other of the town's three thousand inhabitants were paying—and these men knew, when doing it, there could be no redress for us, and no appeal. And for what was it done? Because we refused to give them any more money till they allowed us to stand on an equality with themselves. No such deed as this has ever been done, to our knowledge, since the declaration of independence, making that instrument a nullity.

And how was it looked upon by the men of the nation?—to say nothing of the women —men who possess the same power that you have; for this case has gone from Maine to California and to Oregon, throughout the land, and the men have shown the same spirit of our forefathers of 100 years ago, when they declared on a like occasion that "resistance to tyrants is obedience to God." They have shown their belief in that doctrine by not only assisting us at once, but giving us every assurance to stand by us "to the bitter end." For we are standing, they say, on the foundation on which all our liberties are built that "taxation without representation is tyranny," and "governments derive their just powers from the consent of the governed." Will this spirit ever be put down? It was not put down, 100 years ago, and there is no probability it can ever be done at this time. To make a distinction between mankind and womankind, when one cannot exist without the other, that man should take all the great privileges and allow her no share, but her money must be taken to pay all the expenses of these privileges, though she must never enjoy them. The government of this town is supported by her money, while it allows her no pay from the emoluments of its offices. These the men take. It is not wholly contrary to any idea of honor that men profess, to say nothing of honesty, for the men to take the women's money to spend without her participation? —depriving her of every honored right that they would give up their lives rather than lose themselves! Can any low-lived plunder be equal to this?

We pray you, brethren,—for our natural affection still remains,—leave off this plunder, and give unto us our rights,—those rights we have inherited, together with you, "from nature and nature's God,"—the right to the same liberty that you possess, the right to stand on the same platform, to partake with you of the same privileges. We have the same minds, the same intellect. It is intellect that rules the world. Give unto us the comfort of replying to those who offer to speak for us to the king, "We dwell among our own people." God's laws are fulfilled by love,—let man's be so impartial that they can be fulfilled in the same way.

When Abby had finished her speech, which she read in a clear and forcible tone, Julia, who had meanwhile been sitting on the seat of the wagon, rose and made a few remarks in the same vein, taking for her text an abusive postal card she had received, written by an officer of the town, as she believes, though anonymous. Then the two came down from their impromptu platform, and mingled with the crowd that had been listening to them, and which now manifested considerable disposition to discuss the subject in a good-humored way. For the next quarter of an hour there was a curious scene,—the two defenders of woman's rights to the ballot answering a running fire of questions and objections and holding their own right manfully—we should say if they were not women. All the old claims of the opponents of woman suffrage were brought up; one man for instance, told them there weren't half-a-dozen women in town that wanted to vote, to which Abby replied, "Well, let those half-dozen vote, and the rest stay away, if they want to."

LETTER FROM JULIA AND ABBY SMITH.

Dear Friend, Mrs. Stone:—Your letter of sympathy was received last night, and was a solace to our feelings. If we ever needed sympathy, we did so at the trial of yesterday's meeting.

The moderator was a Republican, perhaps the most in favor of taxation without representation of any man in town, and our application to him to be heard was rejected in short metre. "The voting could not be stopped a moment, and we must wait till Fall before we could be allowed to speak, unless it was on the doorsteps."

The crowd on the outside did not seem to believe that they could not stop the voting for twenty minutes or so, but we were not in a mood to apply again. We were then helped into a wagon, and spoke about fifteen minutes, before a crowd of perfect strangers, knowing but one man, a Republican, though our acquaintance is chiefly among that party. Our acquaintances took care not to speak with us or even hear us. After we came down from the wagon we talked some with this man, and could not possibly make him understand but that it belonged to us to pay the town's expenses as much as it did to him, for "we had the same protection

3

as he had," and this he reiterated a dozen times or more.

Another remarked that "if we were robbed should we not be protected ? "

" Certainly," said we, " if from outside, but if you are to have the money, there is no help from robbery."

" Could we shoulder the musket? Must not our property be taken to carry on the war ? Could we work the highways?"

We replied " we could work as well as those did whom we had seen in front of our house, and we would have them fixed very differently too."

" Then," said some one, " you ought to vote."

There was several very respectable looking men, who, from time to time, would say, they thought us wholly right.

Though the town is Democratic, the other party have shown the most bitterness against us, by inserting pieces in the leading Republican papers in Hartford, which we have always taken, threatening to seize our cows again; and only last week there was an article against us of which we will give you a little item.

" The collector, taking counsel of his gallantry, has concluded to give the ladies a few day's grace, after which the war will be commenced in earnest."

We repeated this extract and said : What are the men of Glastonbury going to fight ? Abby Smith or her cows?

We have understood that the subscrbers of the Hartford *Courant* have threatened that their papers would be stopped, if they published anything more from us, therefore we have never since sent any writing there, to be printed, and the other papers in Hartford are all against us.

We are glad the Democrats have succeeded in electing the two representatives to the General Assembly, as they did last year, though one of them is the Collector, for there are no men in the place of better understanding. Though in the matter of the cows, he was the actor, he was incited to it by others, and has never spoken to us harshly upon any occasion, neither have we known any Democrat who has misrepresented us in the papers. The state of the parties is such, that the Republicans think they shall soon win the day in this town, and they want us disposed of, so they may be relieved of the troublesome job.

We were accused, while talking in the outdoor crowd, of being hired by some of the Woman Suffrage Conventions to go on in this way, It was intimated that we had not put all our taxable property into the list. We told them we had been to no Suffrage Convention before we took this stand.

" Then how came we to think of it ? "

" Because it was not right that our money should be taken from us by force, when the men themselves declared that ' governments derived their just powers from the consent of the governed.' We had not consented, and, therefore, we were bound by no law to pay taxes.

We have the comfort of knowing that one of the editors of the Springfield *Republican* was present, to whom Abby gave her speech, to come out in this morning's paper. Also, a reporter of the Hartford *Times* was there, though we did not see him till after we had done speaking. You must see that we did practise self-denial in earnest, yesterday, and came home almost discouraged with with such wholesale injustice in our native town.

We want to return our thanks to those kind friends who have contributed to the Defense Fund in Boston ; it gives us much support, though we have not yet applied for it. We thought we would wait until we had spoken before the Legislature, according to your advice.

Yours,

JULIA AND ABBY SMITH.

Glastonbury, April 7, 1874.

From the Springfield Republican.

ABBY SMITH AND SISTER.

ANOTHER VISIT FROM THE COLLECTOR.

WHAT HE PROPOSES TO DO ABOUT IT.

To the Editor of the Republican :—

GLASTONBURY, Saturday Evening April 11, 1874.

The collector did not call till 3 o'clock, this afternoon, though we had expected him all the week. He inquired if we could not turn out something to him. We said we could not aid him, for nothing could be more wrong than taking our property in this way ; it was doing what he would not be willing should be done to him. He must take what he pleased, we had no power to resist, we were in his hands ; nothing could be more contrary to justice than for men to make laws against us and be their own executors of them, allowing us no appeal, if they took ever so much. He said they did not make the laws ; they were made long ago. But, we replied, men made them, and not women, and we were put wholly under the men of the town ; they were our lords and rulers. We were under no state law, no other law but theirs, and they did not meet but twice a year, when we must speak to them if we ever could, but they had made a gag-law even in a house we had paid more money to build than any voter in it. They had taken our property from us and sold it off at the sign-post, but would not allow us to speak one word before them in our defense. He said they *might* have heard us. We inquired who put in the moderator—a republican—when the town was democratic. He said now it was done differently, he believed by the registrars. We knew, we said, he must have been put in for the occasion; his opposition to our cause being so well known, he could dismiss us more summarily than any other man. We were glad, we told him, the republicans did not get the rule, as they expected, that we were not put under those who had been writing against us all winter. We had learned through them that it was owing to "the collector's gallantry that we had had a few days' more grace when the war would commence in earnest." We would like to inquire what both parties had agreed to fight against—two helpless women, whom they had deprived of all power of resistance before they began! It was true the democrats had not written against us, and had not appeared so bitter as the other side, led on by five men whose names we mentioned. How would this business appear in a few years to all the men of the place, for, no such deeds having been done to women, it would become matter of history, we thought.

When he left, he said he should use us with as much lenity as possible; he should attach our land, which wou'd require to be advertised nine weeks before it was sold, and we ourselves could bid it off if we chose. We asked what part of our land he proposed taking; he answered, he had not decided. He should put the advertisement in the Hartford Weekly Times of next week; movable estate did not require advertising, but real estate did. He had not seen our appeal to the town. Indeed, we might as well have spoken in any other town, as to being heard by its authorities or our acquaintance. We knew none of them but one republican, who talked the most with us, and who could never see but that others should pay as much as himself, whether they had the same privileges or not! There are none that we have heard of that do not condemn the action of the town in not hearing us, and say they could have done it if they would. The collector appears like a man of sense, but he must be devoid of all feelings of humanity if he can go on and attach our property after all we said to him, especially as the tax is perfectly safe. We told him we had hoped they would let us live in peace the rest of our lives, which they had the perfect power to do.

ABBY H. SMITH AND SISTER.

From the *Nantucket Inquirer and Mirror*, **April 4, 1874.**

Correspondence of the Inquirer and Mirror,

A VISIT TO THE MISSES SMITH AND THEIR COWS.

MESSRS. EDITORS:—On a bright day, when it seemed as if winter had got through lingering in the lap of spring, I set out on my journey to the goodly town of Glastonbury, which adjoins my native town; and though I abode in the place of my nativity until that period in which one is supposed to put away childish things, I had never visited this place, and probably never should, if Abby Smith had not decided that taxation without representation was unjust, and so declined to pay her tax.

Glastonbury is a very uncometable town, lying away from any line of steam travel, so I sought the usual mode of conveyance thither, and took my seat in a rumbling, tumbling old stage coach, which pitched and rolled to that extent that a good, staunch steamer, on the rolling billows, would have been tranquility in comparison. As an aid to digestion a stage coach is a success; and taken at proper intevals, especially up and down our New England hills, would obviate the necessity of a family physician, and as a curative property would far excel the Swedish movement system. Country roads, when the frost is coming out of the ground, and immediately after a three days' rain, are not condusive to fast travel; and when I looked down from my height, and saw the wheels buried in mud to the hubs, I understood why the driver never allowed the sharp crack of his whip to be spent on his four trusty horses.

Perhaps it would be in order to apologize for dwelling on the incident of a short ride into the country, with here and there a sprinkling of a few houses, with their old time well-sweeps and the moss-grown buckets; and the trundling up to the various little post-offices, where men, women and children have congregated to look at the passengers, and to wait for the mail; when our horses are treated to a drink all around, and we wait for an adjustment of matters in general; where we hear the first peep of the frogs adown the marshes, and the song of the blue-birds and the early robin, who cocks up his eye and looks about as if to make sure this is the same country he left a few months ago; and the swelling buds away up in the maple trees, that begin to look red against the sky; and the shining pails hung on their great trunks, down which the sap comes trickling, till the youngsters are obliged to drink a long draught, in order to carry the pails home steadily. Yet, on the whole, I will make no apology, for most people have travelled from "Dan to Beersheba;" they took the double express lightning fast line! and saw the valleys, and the lakes, and the falls and the springs, and the great horse-shoe bend, and the under-ground-ways, &c., &c.; and by means of air-brakes were made to stop fifteen minutes at each place, and make a thorough inspection; so that you can't tell them anything about that mode of travel; whereas, a few miles back in the country, where the family tea-kettle is the only thing that is obliged to get up steam, are sights and sounds that they will admit are fresh and new to them.

The setting sun-rays fell aslant on Glastonbury street, lighting up the noble old elm trees, as we drew up in front of a substantial-looking, two-story, white house, with a generous portico in the centre, which seemed to say—come in; as it had for the past one hundred and thirty-six years; and when the two sisters came out to meet me with extended hands, I must admit, at the risk of appearing old-fashioned, there seemed more hospitality in it than when Bridget goes up and consumes ten minutes to find if her mistress is in.

Seated at the tea-table with Miss Julia and Miss Abby, who were kind'y disposed to regale my mental appetite with the sayings and doings of at least three generations in the past, while at the same time they helped me most bountifully to cream, the like of which I had never seen, save in dreams;—cream from the milk of the veritable Alderneys who were sent up to the sign-post and sold to the highest bidder, (who proved to be the Misses Smith, through their tenant,) was rare enjoyment. From the window opposite we could see the cows, seven in number, who had come up to the bars, and were calling for their evening meal, and as the tenant approached to minister to their wants, I could not resist the temptation of cutting short my repast and without hat, coat or gloves, rushed out to get an introduction to the Alderneys.

"There," said Miss Julia, "is Jessy; she is nine years old, and the mother of them all. We raised her from a calf, and she has always been a great milker. Her milk, butter and cheese are known the town over." I stroked her face, and looked into her great honest eyes, and then passed on to an introduction to Daisy, Roxey, Minnie, Bessy, Whitey and Lilly.

"When the cows were levied upon," said Miss Abby, "they were obliged by law to drive them off the premises seven days before the sale took place, and they took them to an empty tobacco-shed just above here, which was so small they were not comfortable, and we could hear them lowing from our door. On the seventh day the constable led Jessy to the sign-post, (the

place of sale) expecting the others to follow, which they did, like cows in good and regular standing as they were, but having to pass by their home, they broke ranks, and when we looked out on a crowd of about two hundred men and boys, headed by a drum, and saw our pet cows doing their best to get away from their persecutors, it was pretty hard, yet we did not feel it right to pay the tax! Then we put on our things and went to the sale, and why there seemed to be such an especial coolness shown us we did not know; but we soon found they had hoped to get a good Alderney cow for a very little money, and saw we had come to prevent our property from being sacrificed."

The farm of the Misses Smith is three miles long, and comprises some fine timber and meadow land. A pretty gothic cottage occupied by the tenant and his family, stands opposite the homestead, and everything denotes thrift and comfort. "You must come here in summer," said Miss Abby, "and see my flowers. We have them in great profusion, and I teach them that they must make their own way in the world, for I sow them all in together, and those that make the greatest effort, and struggle to get up, receive the most attention."

"Over there," said Miss Julia, "is a little log hut, that my sister, the artist, built with her own hands, where she could go by herself and paint. Our oldest sister had something of a mechanical turn of mind, for she made a small boat, and such as it was, sailed it on the river at the foot of the garden." Miss Julia produced a silk bed quilt, of her own make, with *seven thousand* pieces therein; she had also kept a diary in French, for the past thirty years, and had translated the Bible into three different languages. Among the antiquities in the attic was a clock, made by their grandfather, which much reminded me of the old Walter Folger clock.

In my sleeping apartment I had not observed, by the feeble light of the candle, that anything but a comfortable bed awaited me, till I opened my eyes and the bright sunshine fell upon the walls of the room, and I started up and looked about me; for there suspended on every side were the life-size portraits of the five sisters gazing at me! all in the mutton-leg sleeves, the high-back combs, the puffs and ruffs of the olden time:—coming upon me so unexpectedly, and so very true to life-*size*, that whichever way I turned their eyes were bent upon me, I was fain to beat a hasty retreat, when Miss Abby opportunely came to my relief, and in the order of their ages introduced me to the sisters by the following names: Hansey Zephina, Cyrinthia Sacretia, Larilla Aleroyla, Julia Avolina and Abby

Hadassa. "Our parents gave us peculiar names," said she, to which I unhesitatingly concurred.

During the day, the tax-gatherer called, as the March tax had become due. "I suppose you will be ready to pay us the money," said the gentleman. "No," replied the sisters, "we cannot think it would be right to do so: and you will have to do as you think best in the matter;" whereupon that dignitary withdrew with a puzzled countenance. What do you think they will do this time? I asked. "I don't know," said Miss Abby, "our friends advise us to put away the oil paintings that our sister Larilla painted, and which we prize so much (they are really very fine), but we will do nothing of the kind. Here is our house free for them to come in and take what they think is just. We are told that our country is "the home of the free," at the same time the statistics show that there is a larger proportion of women than men, so that the larger number are in bondage! Why should I love *this* country more than another, when I am ignored as a citizen, and my property taken by and for the minority to make laws to bind me?"

Soon a gentleman called, from four miles away, to get information from Miss Julia in regard to an estate which she had settled. What, do you settle estates? I asked, with surprise. "O, I have settled several for parties who were not able to pay for the same; I have done it as a favor;" and though above seventy years of age; and only a woman, her papers were filed away, and she knew just where to put her hand upon anything that was called for.

The afternoon mail brought numerous letters, among which was one from the vice-president of the temperance convention to be held at Springfield the following week, inviting Miss Abby to be present, and to make some remarks on that occasion. "I am a great advocate for temperance," she said, "and that is a subject that lies first and foremost as an inducement for *women* to vote. The bands of praying women will do good only for a short time, but when women vote, there will be such a vote polled for temperance as never was known; and then, having the law on their side, they will not be insulted and spit upon in the streets, by the lower order of men."

But, Messrs. Editors, I have already trespassed upon your space. The robins were singing cheerily, the smell of spring was all around; spring, which quickens into new life the birds, the beasts, the buds, the the sluggish streams, and thrills our hearts with the Creator's goodness, when the ponderous stage rolled up, and bade good-bye to the Misses Smith, the cows, and the little town of Glastonbury.　　　E. V. H.

From the Chicago Tribune.

THE SMITHS OF GLASTONBURY.

South Glastonbury, Conn., Feb. 14, 1874.
To the Editor of the Chicago Tribune:

Sir: Having seen an extract from The Chicago Tribune, giving an inaccurate account of Abby H. Smith and her sister, also of their whole family, and supposing your correspondent to have been misinformed upon the subject, I will endeavor to give you a fair statement of the facts.

First, their names were: Hancy Zephina, Cyrinthea Lucretia, Laurilla Aleroya, Julia Evelina, Abby Hadassa. The last two only are now living.

Their father was a graduate of Yale College, a native of Glastonbury. He was a Congregational clergyman, and was settled in the western part of Connecticut. His name was Zephaniah Hollister Smith. He married, in the town next where he was settled, Hannah Hadassa Hickock, a lady of uncommon literary attainments. She spoke French, and read the Italian language. She was an astronomer, a great reader and writer; and that her time was not wholly devoted to novel-reading is proved by the fact that when she was 70 years old she learned to read her Bible in the original Hebrew. She was not in the least romantic, but was possessed of strong common sense, being, moreover, a person of pure and lovely character and correct habits,—a good wife and mother.

The father moved to his native place several years after his marriage. The mother bought the farm, which descended to the daughters, and there the two sisters now reside. There he studied law with Judge Brace, became a lawyer, and did the law-business of his native town for nearly forty years. He was always a firm believer in the Bible, and was never considered other than an honorable, Christian gentleman.

The mother and daughters were not unlike other ladies, unless, perhaps, in the fact of their possessing superior and uncommon literary attainments.

These ladies have always been considered among the most respectable and honorable of the people of the town. They are correct in manners and morals, and there is nothing strange or peculiar about them, unless high-minded goodness and Christian charity are rather strange.

Miss Smith is as far above feeling the petty jealousy that springs from vanity, as Miss Abby is from being elated by all the notoriety which has come to her unsought. She little thought, when she asked as a favor of her townsmen that they would consider her claim to a share of the liberties which was gained by the efforts of their common forefathers, that she was striking the most telling blow that has been given for woman's freedom. But so it was, and we trust that she will be sustained under all the excitement that her noble action has brought upon her, until she sees the success of her efforts, and reaps her reward in the blessings of free women,— free to do good, and to help men up to a higher plane of statesmanship and political life; for, in enslaving others, men cease to be free. Never, till man gives woman equality before the law, can he taste the true sweetness of freedom.

Now, permit me to ask if you think it the correct mode of waging warfare against a principle to bring forth the names of those relatives who were nearest and dearest to its expounder,— those enwrapped in the sacredness of death,—and to endeavor, by miscalling and misrepresenting them, to turn men's minds from the true point, the worth of the principle?

Would your correspondent like to have this system of attack extended to him?

Had he a father? had he a mother?
Had he a sister? had he a brother?

It would not be difficult for the moneyed power of woman to find means to set in array before him and the world the names miscalled, of all his relatives, and to make false comments upon their religious principles, their manner of life, and to relate the passing words of ignorant gossips, spoken fifty years ago. Nor would it be impossible to find sleuth-hounds in his own city who would follow up your correspondent's track through all his life; and there are plenty of papers devoted to the woman's cause which would give his record to the world. Is it just, say? If not, do not you think an apology is due from him to those noble ladies who have left the seclusion, so dear to those who see the brightness of another world stealing over the shadows of this, to strike yet once more for the right, fearlessly of consequences, and trusting in God?   Respectfully,
         ROSELLA E. BUCKINGHAM.

[Advertisement in Hartford Weekly Times.]

NOTICE.— Levied upon by virtue of warrant delivered to me for the collection of taxes for the town of Glastonbury, and so much will be sold at public auction, on Saturday, the 20th day of June, A. D. 1874, at 2 o'clock p. m., on the premises, the following described property, bounded as follows: North on land of Edward A. Horton, east on land of heirs of Hannah H. Smith, south on land of J. N. Hollister, west on the Connecticut river, containing 15 acres, more or less, of meadow land, being the same real estate set in the name of Hannah H. Smith's heirs, on the Glaston-

bury grand list of 1873, as will pay the following named tax levied thereon and the cost of collection, namely a tax of 5 mills on the dollar, made due and payable on the first day of March, A. D. 1874.
         G. C. ANDREWS, Collector.
Glastonbury, April 13, 1874.

From the Boston Herald, January 22, 1874.
ABBY SMITH'S COWS.

Abby Smith's cows are bound to take their place in history with Caligula's horse, the goose that by its cackling saved Rome, the wolf that suckled Romulus and Remus, and the ass that spoke for Balaam. There is no help for it. The sisters Smith of Glastonbury, Conn., have a good grievance with which to stand in the gap on the woman suffrage question, and, with their Jersey cows, they make a strong team. Abby Smith is rich in this world's goods. Cows are not her only possession. It is not a case of one little ewe lamb. The Smith girls have houses and bonds and shares and other property lying about so loose that the assessors could not overlook them if he would. But still Abby Smith was not happy. Why was Abby Smith discontented with her lot? Did she mourn her maiden state? No, she rejoices in single blessedness. Did she wish she were a man? No; she thinks men are horrid, not to be thought of by the side of cows, especially her pet Jerseys. Did she lack the comforts, even the luxuries of life? No; she and her cows lived in clover. Did she mourn the lack of accomplishments? Why, she can tell her grievance in four or five different languages, and for ought we know she can sing like a siren and play like Orpheus. None of these things made Abby Smith unhappy. But she couldn't vote! If she could do that little thing, which so many who can neglect to do. there would be no trouble. As she couldn't vote she refused to pay taxes. She and her sister resolved themselves into a Boston tea-party, and declared their sentiments to be: "Millions for defence, but not a cent for tribute;" "Taxation without representation is tyranny;" "he (she) never fails who fails in a just cause," etc. The inexorable collector, a plodding man, devoid of sentiment, under bonds to collect the taxes, ran against this new Declaration of Independence in the performance of his duty. In choosing between the several horns of the dilemma he took seven pairs of horns, with cows attached, which belonged to Abby, some of her own bringing up, and drove them off to pound. Abby Smith felt sad to see her cows go away, harrassed by a drover and a dog, but with that same Spartan spirit which enabled Artemas Ward to cast all his wife's relations on the altar of his country, she restrained her tears and said: "Perish cows for the cause. Thus I will be true to the cause for cows!" The cows were sold at auction, four of them, to satisfy the rapacious tax collector, and we were glad to know that Abby Smith's agent bought them in. They are again complacently chewing their cuds in Abby Smith's comfortable barn, but the case has given a tough cud to the country to chew upon until the new Declaration of Independence is achieved and Abby Smith votes.

LETTER FROM THE SISTERS SMITH.

GLASTONBURY, CONN., April 19, 1874.

Mrs. L. H. Stone: Michigan.

OUR DEAR FRIEND.—Your very friendly letter and kind invitation to be present with you at the suffrage meeting the 6th of May, which we received Friday night, touched our hearts, and we felt so much inclined to go that we spent the rest of the evening in talking over the matter. Could we think ourselves of importance enough to sway a cause of such incalculable consequence, perhaps we should give up everything which personally concerns us, and undertake a longer journey than ever we did in all our lives. But we have come into public notice for such a short time and so wholly unexpected to ourselves, that we can but think that the little we have done is too highly appreciated. When such noble communications come into our hands from the best and most highly educated men and women of the land, with promises to aid us to the utmost, we say to each other, "Can it be that we deserve it?" The morning after we received your interesting letter (the paper sent has not arrived), we were inexpressibly surprised by seeing an advertisement in the Hartford *Times*, printed seven miles from here, which attaches all our meadow land, 15 acres, for the small sum of $49.83, to be sold at auction on the 20th of June, for the second tax, which was claimed to be due the 1st of March. They knew how much our feelings were hurt by the seizure of our cows, and they knew perfectly well that it must touch us to the quick to take away their keeping, for the time is set just before they cut the grass, so that nothing can be left to own but one cow, the poor man's portion. Of all things, we dread another auction, where we suppose the men will want to get the land for as little as they did the cows. We, of course, shall attend the sale, it is not so far off as the sign, being within a few rods of our barn. Then a speech is being prepared to be delivered before the new Legislature, which sits the same day of your meeting, the 6th of May, where we intend to send a petition to be heard sometime during the session, but they may take pattern after our town and deny us a hearing, for Connecticut has always been very backward in reforms. She was the last of the New England States to admit the negroes to vote, and has now some of the worst laws on her statute books for married women of any in the Union. But we do not despond, "for a faint heart never won a fair lady," as we told the outsiders of the town meeting last October, when they put us off by making a rule that there should be no speaking, and we were forced to wait a month until the first speech was made, the 5th of November last, which made such a hub-bub throughout the land. It made a rout from Maine to California, and we have even heard of it in Europe, much to our astonishment. We then thought little of what result we were coming to, but are now more and more convinced of the right of our cause, and can take no backward step as long as our health and life are spared. We are told by some of our townsmen that the speech was a very good one, but we were foolish not to pay our taxes, but doing, we find, has more effect than talking, for what cared they if they could get our money as easily as they had done. We have been misrepresented in the papers as having more property and paying higher taxes than any one else in town. It is not so. Many have more property, but we pay more money into the treasury than any voter, because they work out their taxes or have office, and get orders upon the town, and the money comes principally from the women, who are obliged to earn it hardly enough. There was no need of the town making us so great extra expense as they do, for they could just as well have waited and let the November and March tax come together, for they could get 12 per cent, out of us any way. If they had had but one attachment, it would have saved half the expense of collecting, but it is done to bring us down. Unknown friends have sent us money to indemnify us for extra expense, so that we should not be impoverished by the town's exactions, but we have used none of the drafts and orders yet, and have meant to return it to the generous donors, but we cannot tell yet what we may be driven to do. We have been advised to use it to employ eminent counsel before the Legislature, but we think those who suffer the grievance know better how to state it. We do hate to say we cannot be with you at your meeting, week after next, our feelings are so much interested, and we do want that Michigan should be the banner State. We hope that you will send us a newspaper, containing the account of the proceedings at the meeting in Lansing, for we presume your papers are more liberal than those in

Hartford. The principal Republican paper which we have always taken, and do now, according to report has been threatened that if it printed any more letters from us the subscribers would stop their papers; and the other side will not publish anything upon Woman Suffrage at all. We have several letters on hand to answer that are of an earlier date, but affairs in your State take such a strong hold upon our feelings that we could not refrain from writing to you first.

With heartfelt thanks for your invitation, and much love from both. Yours.

ABBY H. SMITH AND SISTER.

———

For the Advertiser.

A VISIT TO "ABBY SMITH AND HER COWS."

BY MRS. E. LOUISA MATHER.

The 11th of May will ever be a "whiter letter" day with me, for, on that pleasant May morning, early, my friend and self, attended by a Glastonbury friend, started for the home of the famous sisters. Being so early in the day, I feared that we intruded; but soon those fears fled like the dew before the rays of the sun. What genuine hospitality and courtesy were evinced, and what a home! It reminded us of the descriptions of ancient manor-houses, with the notable exception, that there is no privileged ghost to wander in the spacious rooms, or on the lawn of the ancient home of the Glastonbury sisters. No skeleton in the closet, either,—although something quite as unpleasant, was it, when the cherished Alderneys were relentlessly taken away, by the tyranny of the town officials. Julia, the eldest, remarked facetiously, that her sister was *Ally* but *she* was the *cows*, as she is their owner; and, by the way, I partook of cheese at dinner time, made from their milk, which I esteemed a special favor. Julia also narrated many pleasant things that transpired, when they went to Worcester to "aid and comfort" Abby Kelly Foster and companions. And Abby read us a poem in the "Old and New," alluding to the sisters under fictitious names: a witty production, which elicited many a hearty laugh from them and all of us, during the reading. Indeed, it makes not the least difference with them, whether a reporter burlesques them or not; and it all helps on the cause and keeps the ball rolling. She also read her mother's production, for *she* was a poetess, with ready wit and feeling, and likewise a good mathematician. We had the privilege of reading the letters of Mr. Lawrence, of Boston, of a South Carolina lawyer and other notables. Very pleasant was it to roam through the spacious apartments and view the beautiful paintings of the artist-sister, Laurilla. Would that my pen could

well describe them, and their subjects, historical and mythological also, their sanctum, with its flowers and books and paintings, and the round table covered with papers and letters, under the west window, with its outlook on the Connecticut, and on those green meadows, which I suppose will be sold at auction, June 20th, in default of their paying the taxes, which of course, they will never pay, for, "resistance to tyrants is obedience to God." We saw the portraits of the parents—also, those of the five sisters in Abby's chamber—the same room, I believe, occupied by Susan B. Anthony, when in Glastonbury. We also saw Julia's room, and her Bible translations, which were done in that same pleasant chamber. We also passed through the room of the three sisters and of the parents, long since "passed on" to the eternal home. Last, but not least, we ascended to the attic, and saw Julia's cradle where she slept in her infancy, the little chair in which she sat as a child, and also some of her mother's manuscript, besides many other interesting things which we have not time to describe. Commend us to a garret for enjoyment, any time, — but especially to *this* one. Out doors we went on the lawn and in the garden, which must be very beautiful in the season of flowers. With reluctance, we left, in the afternoon, this delightful home, which had seen the sunshine and showers of 130 years, uniting the beauty and use of the old, with the conveniences of the new,—even as the sisters, with "the grand, old name" of lady, seem a cheerful blending of the past, with its joys, pleasures and customs; and the present, with its noble views and eliminations of truth, adjusted to the needs of the age. The sisters and their home will have a prominent place in the future annals of the country. And, in that "good time coming," when woman no more shall be the sport and victim of tyrannical laws and customs—when, free to act, she performs her share in the formation of government, the story will be told to children, in the gloaming, or by the fireside, of Julia and Abby Smith's cows, and their unflinching resistance to injustice and oppression.

HADLYME, CONN.

From the New Haven Evening Union, June 3, 1874.

———

HEARING BEFORE THE COMMITTEE ON WOMAN SUFFRAGE.

———

MISS ABBY SMITH'S ADDRESS.

The Committee on Woman Suffrage gave a hearing on that question this afternoon in room No. 14, Insurance Building. The room was crowded, the larger portion of the audience being gentlemen.

Mr. Joseph Sheldon first spoke in support of the movement, making a short and pointed address at the close of which he introduced Miss Abby Smith. In his remarks the gentleman brought up by way of argument, the instance of the negroes of the South, who it appeared—no matter how degraded they are—enjoy the privileges of freedom to a fuller extent than thousands of intelligent women. Miss Abby Smith and sister then came forward arguing as follows :

We would thank you, gentlemen, for the indulgence you have shown us in permitting us to set forth our grievances before you, well-knowing that we who have felt those grievances can tell them with more effect than others can do it, however eloquent. We feel the more thankful for this privilege having been so lately denied it in our own town We are peaceful citizens of this the native State of all our ancestors, and we the last of our family, having been brought up on its soil, and spending our whole lives in its very midst. No spot is so dear to us, no name that we love so well. And why do we not love its laws and institutions, its customs, and manners? Because its government has made two classes among its citizens—a superior and an inferior class—and we belong to the inferior one. She has established a caste among us, founded on birth, for which we are not to blame, and could not possibly control, and from which like the East Indians we can never rise, whatever may be our ability or attainments This distinction is more cruel than that of the same kind in India, because we are living with our superiors, and therefore more enlightened, and can feel more keenly its injustice, its opposition to every rule of right, of reason, and of common sense. The government of this State affords us of the inferior class no protection from its laws, though it takes our money to pay for the support of those laws, made wholly for the benefit of the superior class. The State instead of providing for the weak and defenceless for which governments are instituted, have given up all such into the hands of the strong and powerful, in the places where they live, to deal with them as they choose, without any appeal or redress! To the superior class the State has given permission to take our money from us, the lower order, whenever they may agree to do so, whenever they choose to take it, and as much as they choose to take, without ever giving us the least voice in the matter. If we, the owners, refuse to give it, they seize what we value the most and sell it at the public sign-post, knowing they are accountable to none for their deeds; if we desire to

speak in our own defence, when they assembled together, we are at once denied the privilege, even in a house for the erection of which they had taken more money from us than from any of the men assembled in it.

When God created man in his own image, for "in the image of God created He him, male and female created He them," He gave *them* dominion over what? Not over one another; not over their own kind, but over the birds of the air and the fishes of the sea, after their kind, and over the cattle of the earth, and whatsoever creepeth on the face of the earth, after their kind. And is man served among these animals more by the males than by the females? Does he make a distinction on account of sex? Does he not allow one the same privileges of the same kind that he allows the other—the same freedom? Does he ever find these animals, in their natural state, the males congregating together excluding the females? And how does he obtain his dominion over them? Not by physical strength, for theirs, many times is greater than his, but by his intellect, which God has given him greater than theirs. But it is physical strength by which he rules over woman, putting her in a situation which he calls her sphere, and confining her there because he is the strongest; allowing her no participation in what he values the highest; in what he calls his God given rights, which he has inherited from "Nature and Nature's God," and takes her money to enable him to maintain these rights, not seeing that she has inherited the same rights from the same source. Can woman, of the same kind as man, be ruled over in this way without feeling his degradation? You may indulge her by every means in your power, and give her the highest education possible, it only makes her feel the wrong the more deeply, for she sees she can have no scope for her talents; she can never put her attainments into practise. She desires the same liberty that you possess—the same freedom. Better far for her to have remained under England, where she stood on an equality with the men. She did no little then in assisting him to gain his freedom, not deeming that his freedom was her bondage, for he can now rule over her with irresponsible sway. Independence for man was a sad day for women. They have been going downward ever since.

The State in her ministrations has never considered the welfare of half her citizens —her woman—for they having no voice in framing her laws, and no power, the men thought of what use would be rights and privileges to her, they could take care of the women and provide all things necessary for them. This is the slaveholder's logic, also of the State of Connecticut. Women have no rights that the men are bound to respect. This half of her citizens, whom the State has disfranchised, she obliges to pay equally and perhaps more for all her institutions and improvements, though she can have none of its offices or emoluments; these belong to the superior class. The women are more honest than the men. They are moral; better citizens. They are never seen round the grogshops, and therefore makes the State very little trouble and expense in comparison to the men. Should she, with her small earnings, be taxed for the men's bad conduct, for those great and expensive buildings erected to confine the men for disturbing the public peace? There are but two women in our State's Prison and 228 men. The women suffer the most from drink in their houses but could the man know that his wife could vote against his getting it, it would restrain him even in his maddened moments. What peace would that alone bring to nearly half the inhabitants of the State? Can the men of this State prosper who have thus forsworn and repudiated the very principles on which they based their claims,when they separated from the mother country, making the most solemn asseverations to the justice of their claims, before the face of the whole world, founded as they said on natural rights, that government derive their just powers from the consent of the governed and taxation without representation is tyranny? Can these men that govern our State go so directly contrary to their own doctrines that they have sworn to support, without incurring the penalty affixed to the transgression of the moral law ? What did they suffer from Great Britain beyond the seas, to what the women suffer now in half the houses of this land from brutal men who claim the right to tyranism over their own families? But have they already gone on with impunity in degrading their own mothers, wives and daughters, to a state that they feel no interest in the affairs of government, having no voice in the matter? There is nothing in this world that concerns the inhabitants of every land where they live, men and women alike so much as does the government of that land. As the laws are administered in justice and impartiality, in imitation of the laws of our maker, that land will prosper, and nothing will prosper if they are not. In vain we labor for it. It requires mind, deep thought and contrivance to accomplish the greatest of all earthly good; not only of the men, but of the women; for if man degrade woman, her intellect and his intellect will suffer also; for he is of the woman and from the woman, and he cannot exist without her. In whatever situation in life

he places her, with or without intellect, he must descend to her level. He has taken from her all interest in the affairs of government, determined to carry on that business alone, (rejecting family government, instituted in the beginning of the earth, where all the members are equally cared for), and what is the consequence? Look at the women of the land as they are ruled by the men instead of being ruled by the laws. Are they not wholly given up to dress and outside show, which requires no mind, no intellect? And look at the men also—our Congress, the highest court in the country—are they not also wholly given up to obtaining the means to gratify the outward desires of themselves and their families? Does mind rule in that body? And we all know that without that the outward prosperity will soon perish. We pray you gentlemen to cast away your heathen code of laws, founded on birth, instead of justice, and frame your laws as the laws of your Maker are framed, where there is neither bond or free, male or female. God having from the beginning made both of one flesh, and all the inhabitants of the earth stand alike in his sight. God has made of one blood all nations of men, to dwell on all the face of the earth, and made but one law for their government; and he that obeys that law shall live by it, and he that disobeys it shall be punished by it. Does he mean men alone or has he included women also? Why does man need but one law for the government of both? In view of all these considerations we pray that equal rights may be accorded to us according to the Fourteenth Amendment of the United States Constitution, which says *all persons* born or naturalized in the United States and subject to the jurisdiction thereof, are *citizens* of the United States, and of the State in which they reside. No State shall make or enforce any law which shall abridge any privileges or immunities of the citizens of the United States, nor shall any State deprive *any person* of life, liberty or property without this process of law, nor deny to any person within its jurisdiction the equal protection of the laws. And have we had equal protection of the laws? when our property can be taken from us at any time without our having any voice in the matter. Can any reason be given why it is not as wrong to take money in this way from a woman as it would be from a man, and as contrary to all this country's boasted laws of freedom?

From the Hartford Times.

A WORK OF ART FROM A COW'S TAIL.

We were shown yesterday a little work of art, unique and complete in its way, a duplicate of which has been put in the Union Bazaar. It is a boquet made of the hair of the famous Alderney cows belonging to Abby Smith and sister. These two bouquets were made by Miss Emma V. Hallet of South Manchester, who visited the Smith sisters some months ago and divested the cows' tails of sufficient hair for this purpose, presenting one of the bouquets to Miss Smith and the other to the Bazaar. The original number of these celebrated Alderneys was seven. Two have been sold, so five are represented in the bouquet. The hair of Jessy, the grandmother of the flock, is made into a jasmine. Daisy and Minny are her children, and the hair of Daisy being of a suitable color, forms a bunch of daisies, the resemblance being complete. Roxey and Whitey are Jessy's grandchildren, Roxey's hair being made into cowslips, and Whitey's into buttercups—cowslips and buttercups—names very fitting for the occasion, and the flowers very beautifully made. The whole bouquet shows great skill in the making, and the idea connected with it is neatly and artistically carried out by its being tied with streamers of black ribbon, on which, in gilt letters is printed the revolutionary cry: "Taxation without representation." The following letter accompanies the bouquet:

GLASTONBURY, June 8, 1874.

Our Dear Friend, Miss HALLETT

How can we express our thanks to you for such a wonderful specimen of skill. We are sure this beautiful present ought to recompense us, if anything could, for the trial of seeing our pet Alderneys, without any fault of theirs, held in durance vile seven days, driven to the sign-post to be sacrificed to the highest bidder.

ABBY SMITH AND SISTER.

There will be no difficulty in disposing of the Alderney bouquets in the bazaar. Doubtless fifty of them put on sale there —if the Jessies and Dasies could hold out like the Charter Oak—would sell off like hot cakes.

From the New Haven Union, June 1874.

To the Editor:

We have just returned from an auction sale, or rather no sale, of our meadows, which resulted in measuring off eleven acres of the land for a tax of $29.83, and sold for $78.35, which the collector said was the amount of the tax and the cost. We had consulted two eminent lawyers in Hartford, who told us that the law expressly said that movable estate must be levied upon first, and that land could not be taken if personal property could be found, and there was a sufficiency without levying upon real estate. According to the advertisement we were on the ground at two o'clock, and told the collector, after waiting an hour from the time set, that it was unlawful to sell it. He said it was already bargained for, but if we wished to bid we could. We told him that would be consenting to an unlawful deed, and that men ought to obey laws they had made themselves, before forcing women to do it; but we could have no effect, and after calling out twice for another bid, he, Judge Hunt like, struck it off. We asked to whom, he said Mr. H., a man who bought a farm next north of us, some twenty years ago, and who has been trying to get our land by moving bounds between us, and other outrageous acts, so that there was no living beside him without going to law. It is quite a comfort to us that the collector could not get another one to bid, that had money to pay for the land, for it shows that the reputable men of the town did not countenance such a low-lived act. It is well known by everybody here that our bad neighbor has injured us all he could, and was only restrained by the law, and the collector well knew it, too. Mr. H. and three others to measure off the eleven acres, were all that were there, except two of our neighbors who accompanied us, and not one of us heard the land bid off at all. It must have been done before our premises were reached, and the advertisement said it was to be sold on the premises. We have now but four acres of meadow land left, and the poorest part too. Meadow land sells for $150 to $200 per acre, so that nearly $2,000 worth was disposed of for $78.35. There is nobody that would dare go on and cut the grass from so unlawful a sale but Mr. H., and our two neighbors are much afraid that he will do it. We have promised them the getting of the hay, and they are depending upon it. We are intending to go to Hartford as soon as possible, but fear our lawyer (Mr. J.) will be gone, as he was last week when we called on the ex-mayor, who gave us the same reading of the law. This is a deed that we could not have believed even the man that so ruthlessly seized our cows could have been persuaded to do. There may be a sequel to this sad story which will give more interest.

ABBY SMITH AND SISTER.

Glastonbury, June 20, 1874.

From the Springfield Republican.

LETTER FROM BOSTON TO FORNEY'S PAPER PHILADELPHIA.

I close this Suffrage demonstration by a salute to Abby H. Smith of Glastonbury, Conn., and the cows which the town authorities took because she refused to pay her taxes until she could have a vote in town affairs. The salute is in the form of a letter from one of our most wealthy and conservative citizens, who seems to have learned more from the sale of those cows than some of our legislators have from all sources within their reach. The letter, although written soon after the occurrence, has recently appeared in print. Mr. Lawrence's facts and figures are suggestive.

MR. LAWRENCE'S LETTER.

BROOKLINE, Jan. 14, 1874.

MY DEAR MADAM:—The account of your hardships is interesting, and your action will be highly beneficial in bringing the subject to public notice, and in leading to the correction of a great injustice. The taxation of the property of women with out allowing them any representation, even in town affairs, is so unfair that it seems only necessary to bring it to public view to make it odious and to bring about a change. Therefore, you deserve the great honor, not only because you have suffered in a good cause, but because you have set an example that will be followed, and that will lead to happy results. Your case has its parallel in every township of New England. In the town where this is written a widow pays into the town treasury $7,830 a year, while six hundred men, a number equal to half the whole number of voters, pay $1.20 in all. Another lady pays $5.42. Yet neither has a single vote, not even by proxy. That is, each one of six hundred men who have no property, who pay only a poll-tax, and many of whom cannot read or write have the power of voting away the property of the town, while the female owners have no power at all. We have lately spent a day in celebrating the heroism of those who threw overboard the tea; but how trifling was the tea-tax, and how small the injustice to individuals, compared with this one of our day! The principle, however, was the same—that there should be no taxation where there is no representation. And this is what we ought to stand by. Please to accept the sympathy and respect of one of your fellow citizens. No doubt you will have it from all in due time, or, at any rate, from all who love to see fair play.

Very truly yours,
AMOS A. LAWRENCE.

MISS ABBY H. SMITH, Glastonbury, Conn.
HOWARD.

From the Woman's Journal, July 11, 1874.

After music by the band, the sisters Smith were loudly called for, and came forward together to the platform amid hearty applause.

MISS JULIA SMITH, of Glastonbury, gave an interesting account of the seizure of her sister's cows, and the treatment she has received at the hands of the officers. She described with artless simplicity the surprise the sisters felt, when they found their names suddenly conspicuous in the newspapers, and an unexpected conflict thrust upon them by their fellow townsmen.

MISS ABBY SMITH then spoke as follows:

SPEECH OF ABBY SMITH.

We often hear it observed, "My money is as good as anybody's," meaning they can get the same privileges for the same amount, whatever their outward appearance. This is the received opinion everywhere, that money is of the same value let who will hold it. This is justice and is the rule in all our dealings with each other, that our money should bring an equivalent. But in Connecticut, where we have always lived, it is different. There, they take the money of those who cannot defend it, whenever they get a chance, without any equivalent whatever. We have had, in that State, a great deal of money taken from us in this way, without the least pretence of its

going for any advantage of ours, and we never see or hear from it again. The government there sanctions such doings; if they can only get at the money to maintain their power, they care not how, nor from whom, and never think of giving the owners the least benefit from it.

I know not how to address an assembly like this, who hold to the same truths that we do, for these truths are all so perfectly self-evident, and have been looked over, this one hundred years, by all the great men of the country, and are so fully established that one like myself, not used to speaking, could not be expected to add a new idea. But, last November, seeing our fellow townsmen going so contrary to these truths, never questioned by anybody, and so contrary, too, to every idea of what we all hold to be right, I thought I would just tell them of it, and, though my sister warned me of the consequences, I still believed they would consider our position and try to excuse themselves to us in the best way they could. But, though they gave us the most strict attention, while we were speaking, they never said a word when we were through (nor afterwards, so far as we could learn), but went on with their other business, as before, and we knew nothing how they felt till they took our cows.

I seem to be particularly unfortunate in all my three speeches (I never made but three), as to pleasing my audience, which all desire to do. The second time I attempted to speak we were turned out of doors, and out there, what I said did not suit any better, for they attached all our meadow land after it. But we thought the Legislature would be more enlightened than our town meetings, and the Committee did seem to give due consideration to what we said, but they did not look over well suited, and they never applauded us at all as they did the two that spoke afterward. But these two were married women and they probably knew how to please the men better than we ever could. The State has given us no answer as yet, which looks as if it meant to continue its tyranny over the helpless. And this morning, since we took the cars to come here, we see by the newspapers that Legislature has "given us leave to withdraw."

The sisters sat down amid the heartiest applause.

From the Woman's Journal.

THE SISTERS SMITH'S COWS.

To the men of Glastonbury. July 4, 1874

Forced from our gentle mistress' yard,
Her generous feed and friendly " card,"
Our case, though not above all others hard,
Is yet remarkable in this regard—
That, unintelligent and dumb,

We're made to suffer martyrdom
For our good mistress, in her cause,
And testify against your laws,
    O men of Glastonbury!

Our lowings deep, in exile bound,
Shall yet be heard the world around,
Our frantic bellowings proclaim
The wrongs of Woman and your shame;
Proclaim, so far as justice goes,
Ye are the age's Pharaohs,
    Ye lords of Glastonbury!

In seventeen hundred and seventy-three,
Your grandmothers gave up their tea,
Their husbands threw it in the sea,
Protesting against tyranny.
Their granddaughters your tax resist,
Demanding justice at your hands,
A place upon your voting list;
Ye sell their houses and their lands,
Their household treasures and their pets,
To pay your town's dishonest debts,
    O men of Glastonbury!

Have you forgotten Lexington?
And Putnam brave, your gallant son?
And all the battles fought and won?
Fought not your sires for equal rights,
For righteous laws and life's delights?
    O men of Glastonbury!

Your bells clang out from yonder towers,
Your cannon boom the passing hours;
Your orators of noble fame
Shout eulogies on Woman's name;
From public halls your banners stream,
From broad escutcheons eagles scream;
To-night your votive fires will gleam,
Yet only mockeries do they seem,
    O men of Glastonbury!

Ye boast of your superior parts,
Of gallantry and loyal hearts,
Yet make your women speak from carts,
Outside your halls. Yet not unheard
The everlasting, living word
Of justice—for the very stones
Trumpet your wrong in thunder tones,
    O men of Glastonbury!

Misguided men of Glastonbury!
'Tis meet that while ye feel so strong
Ye fill the measure of your wrong;
Ceaseless and slow the mills of fate
Grind on and on, and soon or late,
There cometh to all the even scale,
And righteous judgment doth not fail.
Ye, without color or just cause
Do execute your cruel laws,
With mock devotion shut your eyes,
And, clothed in smooth hypocrisies,
Make loud professions to your God,
The while your women ye defraud,
    O men of Glastonbury!

In coming time, when all is past,
And cruel reign of sex and caste
Is at an end, and men unite
To give to womankind their right,
It will not be your glory then
That ye were Glastonbury men,
Who voted to deny your wives
The greatest blessing of your lives.
Ah no! alas! the very name
Of Glastonbury shall inflame
The noble indignation pent
In patriot souls, and each event—
Each now unnoticed incident,
Shall live in history to your shame,
    O men of Glastonbury!
           A. Briggs Davis.

*From the Springfield Republican, Sept. 5,
1874.*

THE SMITH SISTERS, AGAIN.

From Our Special Reporter.

Glastonbury, Ct., Friday, September 4.

Rural Glastonbury has had the monotony
of its quiet existence stirred a little, to-day,
by another exhibition of the pluck of the
Smith sisters in their contest with the mas-
culine oppressors of womankind. The
theater of this local sensation was the house
of Justice Hollister in the southern portion
of the town, and the occasion the trial of
the suit brought by the famous sisters
against the tax-collector, for trespass upon
a certain meadow of theirs which was sold
by him in June, illegally, as they claim, to
pay delinquent taxes.

Since their vigorous proceedings in behalf
of woman's right to the ballot, last fall, the
sisters have acquired a great local as well
as national fame, and from the crossing of
Connecticut at Hartford to their homes,
eight miles away, anybody will promptly
give the most minute directions to the
stranger inquiring his way to their dwelling.
The long straggling village street of Glastonbury was as quiet and vacant, this morning, as Goldsmith's deserted village. Not
even a cat or a dog was to be seen; the
front blinds of the antiquated houses that
lined the way were hermetically sealed,
and excavated Pompeii could hardly convey
a more vivid impression of solitude and
desertion to the passer-by than this
village street. An exploration into the
rear of any of these dwellings, however,
would speedily correct this notion. The
back kitchens teemed with busy life, as we
found in our occasional endeavors to con-
vince ourselves of the existence of human
beings in this Rip Van Winkle town. At
one ample homestead we found the farmer
occupants philosophically splashing the
dasher of a great barrel churn in a monoto-
nous up-and-down fashion, while his wife
contentedly sat by preparing the family
dinner. Evidently she believed it a mild
form of woman's rights, at least, and that
churning is not one of the inalienable privileges of womankind, as is so often the
case in country districts. Both were alert
regarding the redoubtable Smith sisters,
and only regretted that they had not donned
their armor for the unequal fight with
mankind at a more youthful period of their
existence.

Approaching Justice Hollister's, a little
off the main street, there were signs of
people stirring about. In front of the house
stood a row of teams, betokening some un-
wonted occurrence within. The inside
itself presented a bit of picturesque group-
ings worthy the brush of a Hogarth.
Through an ample hall-way opened the
sitting-room, connected with yet another
room by folding doors. In the latter,
around a table, sat those immediately interested in the case. The justice of the
peace, an exceedingly quiet, home-spun
gentleman, with short, gray hair, occupied
the most conspicuous place, and chewed a
lead-pencil and nervously rubbed his chin

as the lawyers with flattering unction sandwiched in their "your honors." Flanking him on either side were the attorneys for the plaintiff and defendant, shrewd and tenacious, and both deeply versed in the noble art of bothering and befogging witnesses. Grouped about were the principal witnesses, the unlucky tax-collector, tall and angular—a good specimen of the modern Yankee—the surveyor and his assistants, who measured off the disputed land, various town officials, with countenances expressive of grave interest, and last, but not least, the two heroines of the play. They are dressed in prim but genteel black, and sit beside each other, keenly watching the slow unfolding of the plot. Abby is the taller of the two, thin and straight as a lath, and sits erect in her cane-bottomed chair through the tedious hours with less signs of weariness than a modern girl in her teens would show. Julia, the elder, is more petite, and shows less indications of age, if anything, than her sister. Notwithstanding she is nearly 80 years, her face is still bright and expressive, and she evidently entered into the occasional humors of the affair more heartily than Abby. At first, both were restive under the hatcheling of the cross-examination and the petty sparring of the lawyers, and uttered an impatient protest, but as the hours wore on, they settled down into heroic resignation.

But the gathering of the town-folks in the outer room contained the most motley features of the scene. These spectators were ranged on uncomfortable wooden benches, and numbered some 20 or more of the sterner sex. Indeed, the only women present to countenance the sisters were one matronly witness and a couple of young ladies, who furtively listened to proceedings through the open door of an adjoining parlor. The rows on the benches consisted of farmers in their shirt-sleeves, fresh from the rowen field and the potato patch. The miller, well powered with flour, edged his way in for an entertaining and profitable nooning. Several small boys and embarrassed youths, with clean paper-collars atop of soiled shirts, looked on with awe-struck countenances, and consoled themselves with peanuts on the sly during the earlier intervals. Indeed, the awesome way with which the spectators, both young and old, evinced their sense of the majesty of the law was quite oppressive. It was contagious, and a thoughtless little black-and-tan terrier, that strayed into the court, slunk guiltily under a bench beneath the influence. The ticking of a clock in a neighboring room became painfully audible at times, and the chance to smile or laugh at the sparsely scattered jokes of the legal gentlemen afforded intense relief.

But to the points of the case itself. As mentioned above, the suit was brought by the Smith sisters against Tax-Collector Andrews for trespass on their meadow land, last June, in selling it illegally, as they claim, for unpaid taxes. The taxes and expenses amounted to a matter of $80, and, instead of levying on movable property, as the law directs, the incautious or ignorant collector proceeded to sell to Nelson A. Harding eleven acres of meadow valued at $4500 for the trifling amount of the taxes. This, notwithstanding the protest of the sisters on the ground at the time of the sale. The neighbor to whom the land was sold has long been a thorn in the flesh of the sisters, bothering them in various ways through a long period of years, and this fact only added fuel to their determination to wage the contest to the furthest point. Mr. Horace Cornwall of Hart'ord conducted the case for the Smiths, and W. S. Goslee of Glastonbury represented the defendant. In view of the plainness of the law, however, plainly requiring the sale of movable property for taxes before that of real estate, and the palpable possession of the Smith sisters of more than sufficient movables to liquidate the tax, the defendant had an up-hill job of it, and the justice's verdict in favor of the Misses Smith was only that already anticipated by the town-folks generally. So the unlucky tax-collector has to pay damages of $10 and costs, which, altogether, will considerably lighten the profits of his office for this year at least. The next act in the drama of taxation without representation in the town of Glastonbury will be Tax-Collector Andrews's raid on the furniture of the Smith mansion for the unpaid tax, succeeded by no end of botheration probably to this unfortunate official, and the still further concentration of the popular attention upon the contest the sisters have inaugurated, and are now more than ever resolved to continue.

From the New Haven Evening Union, Sept. 9.

ABBY SMITH'S LETTER.

ALL ABOUT THAT CASE.

To the Editor of the Evening Union.

Some weeks ago an account of the unlawful and outrageous sale of our meadow land to a very bad neighbor was published in your paper, and perhaps your readers might be interested to learn the sequel; the end is beyond our vision. A suit was brought against the collector and tried before the most fair (?) justice of the peace in this town, last Friday, the 4th inst. It was clearly proved that there was abundance of personal estate, and that they could not lawfully touch the real estate; but as it was an action of trespass, only nominal damages could be given, and ten dollars and the costs were awarded. When the facts of the case came out it was shown to be most unlawful and iniquitous. We had a scrutinizing and excellent lawyer, Mr. Cornwall, of Hartford, who made a special examination in the cost paid out for the collection of a tax of less than fifty dollars, and the charges, twenty-eight dollars and fifty-two cents. It was shown clearly that it was all contrived out before the attempted auction. The bill for measuring eighty rods length of land in a straight line, taking the width by hearsay, was six dollars and fifty cents, and the Glastonbury lawyer was allowed three dollars and fifty cents for making the deed, and other unlawful charges were not accounted for. It looked like a conspiracy to get money out of women. Our lawyer said in his plea that the case was more outrageous than he had any idea of before the trial. We were glad that some of our town's people could hear how their women who have always been law-abiding citizens were treated by their native town officials, and who had the collector's assurance before the seizure of their cows, that by paying twelve per cent a year the tax could lay as long as we chose. The collector denied everything we said to him about our personal estate, though our neighbor Mrs. K. was present and testified to its truth. His lawyer, Mr. G., in his plea poured forth a bitter tirade against us personally; there was no argument of law in the case. When he found it was decided in our favor, as every one who heard the testimony knew it must be, he threatened us terribly about the consequences when this tax would be laid again. It would be much worse for us than if we had paid for all this case. We made no reply, but our lawyer told him, unless they went more according to law, it would be difficult to collect any tax. Mr. G. quibbled so in asking unnecessary questions, that we had to sit before the judge from ten in the morning until six in the evening, with only half an hour's intermission given us by the justice. It was a tedious day, but ended entirely to our satisfaction. We have just heard that Mr. G. has appealed the case to the next court at Hartford, which begins its session to-morrow. We do not suppose they will let these wonderful doings ever come to light in Hartford. We think it is done to hold on a year for our bad neighbor to record his deed of two thousand dollars worth of land, which cost him seventy-eight dollars and thirty-five cents.

ABBY H. SMITH AND SISTER.

Glastonbury, Ct., September 7, 1874.

From the Woman's Journal, Sept. 5, 1874.

PERSECUTION OF THE SISTERS SMITH.

EDITORS WOMAN'S JOURNAL: — A few weeks ago you published some account of the unlawful sale of nearly all our meadow land, with very feeling and appropriate remarks. Perhaps your readers would like to learn the sequel, though the end is not yet.

Immediately after the sale, we went to Hartford, seven miles from here, to see our lawyer, who seemed to think the Collector might be prosecuted without fail, for not taking personal estate, (for there was a sufficiency of that), but he was so busy that he wished us to wait a couple of weeks, as our greatest enemy, to whom it was sold, could not cut a clip of the grass.

At the time he set, we went again, and then he said he was engaged before the Legislature in a case between Glastonbury and Wethersfield concerning the boundary line, and we must wait till the rising of the assembly before he could attend to the case, two or three weeks later. We, of course, were at his office in season again, and he appeared somewhat cooler, acknowledging that he had seen the Collector, who is a member of the Legislature, and that the Collector told him we denied having any personal property, (wholly untrue) and he advised us to pay the original tax, for he thought they must have some ground to fall back upon, as we were described as Hannah H. Smith's (our mother's) heirs, and we could inherit but a trifle of movable estate from her, for the principal was derived from our sisters.

We then told him, let that be pleaded; if men would quibble in that way we wanted it to come out, for they stripped us of our cows, as Hannah H. Smith's heirs, and these cows had all been raised since her death, and they could be taken up for that. But he was going to Saratoga the next week, and could do nothing under two weeks more, and he would then see to it.

When he returned, we were again in his office. We called on him at least six times in all, and he promised to do the business each time, except the last, when he wished us to get another lawyer to make out the writ, and he would help him if he wished it. He is of the same politics as the authority of our town, and it will not do to offend voters. We cannot vote.

He told us that the town, in case it was decided against them, would carry it up through every court, even to the court of errors. How did he know this? or did he say it to dishearten us?

We employed other counsel, whom we were sorry we could not have consulted in the first place, but we supposed he was in Europe. We saw him in Hartford on Thursday, and he said he had given a writ to be served on the Collector that day, which must first be tried before a justice of the peace in this town, which will be done on Friday, the 4th of September, at 10 o'clock A. M., and if not decided in our favor, we have no protection under the law. Three different lawyers of Hartford have expounded the law contrary to the doings of the Collector. Of course we shall appeal from an adverse action.

Yours, with respect,
ABBY H. SMITH AND SISTER.
Glastonbury, Conn.

From the Woman's Journal, Oct. 17, 1874.

ABBY H. SMITH'S SPEECH BEFORE THE R. I. SUFFRAGE SOCIETY AT ITS ANNUAL MEETING.

We have been requested to prove the assertion we have often made, that we have no protection from the laws of the land. This we are told is the greatest objection that men make to all we say, that we are surely wrong, for we are protected by them in every way. When we petitioned the Connecticut Legislature last spring, we availed ourselves for the first time of the only right, the right of petition, the State has ever granted us. We prayed to be put on an equality with the other citizens of the State. Instead of our petition being considered and discussed or acted on in any way, we were told we had leave to withdraw. That is, to withdraw all the claim we ever had for the protection of that body, though we are native born citizens of the State and all our ancestors before us, since its first settlement. We stated that we were wholly in the hands of the town to take our property from us whenever they chose, and as much as they chose without any appeal or redress from their doings, and the Legislature of the State have decided that we are. This brings the treatment we receive upon the men of our town where it belongs. We do not see how any warrant can be served again upon us headed by " The Authority of the State of Connecticut," for the State has given up all authority over us, and as the United States' laws are all founded on the principle that "all governments derive their just powers from the consent of the governed," and as

we are not permitted to vote we cannot see that the United States protect us more than any other government. It has occurred to us lately that whatever influences may be exerted by our town officers, they would never have proceeded against us so rigidly, had it not been for the support given them by members of the North Congregational Church. Looking over their proceedings, we find that every man that has come out openly against us in this persecution, without exception, is a member of that church. The Congregational society of our place has ever considered itself of more importance than any other, probably the most wealthy and has the most church members. It professes, of course, to hold the Bible as strongly as we do, but we have never joined with it in its religion, though we have had more friends and associates among its members than in any other sect. We understand the collector is a member of that church, though in the east parish, and the lawyer who has done all the town's business against us, writing, pleading, etc., is a prominent member of the church. The man who turned us out of the town house is another member. Also the one who opposed us the most bitterly after we came out, is another. The surveyor who charged six dollars and fifty cents for measuring off eighty rods of our meadow land in a straight line is another. Our lawyer asked him why he needed two assistants, (having a dollar and a half apice), and he said the law allowed them to him. Our greedy neighbor who bargained for $2000 worth of our meadow land by paying seventy-eight dollars thirty-five cents is another member. We never could do anything with him by reasoning about right and wrong, because he thought himself upheld by the church having considerable property. The man who has written long pieces against us in a Hartford paper is a trading clergyman of the same church, preaching whenever he can get a chance. Another member, a former deacon, said when the case was decided in our favor, that, "We shall support our collector." "Against the law?" he was asked but he only repeated the assertion. Still, another member, a neighbor, refused last fall to bring the WOMAN'S JOURNAL for us from the Post Office as he had done. The members of the church and congregation, many of them our professed friends, can stand by and see two women of our years, well-known to them all, without support from either church or State, about to be robbed of all they possess without one word of disapproval, for it is done by their own members. I say robbed, for the laws of all nations make it as much robbery to take a woman's property from her by force, as to take a man's property from him by force.

None can see the least difference. It is church and State power. There is no power under heaven that has done such deeds of darkness without mercy, and without compunction, as religious power upheld by the State. Jefferson saw this and delivered the men of the country from it, but the women, as this case clearly shows, are yet under it.

We are pleased to come for the first time in our lives to Rhode Island. It has never been ruled by a religious power. Its founder, Roger Williams, was more enlightened than the governors of the neighboring States at that time. He carried out his idea of right, fearing neither church nor State, and by this means rendered himself and this State forever famous.

ABBY H. SMITH.

From the Woman's Journal.

TAXATION WITHOUT REPRESENTATION.

The following address was prepared by Miss Julia E. Smith, of Glastonbury, for the recent Providence Meeting.

Two or three weeks ago, we recieved a letter from a stranger in Illinois. He said he was three score and ten, and he might yet live to be an old man and see women vote. He had advocated this for forty years, and thought it would prevail in less than ten. Though it is not one year since we came before the public, we have suffered no little vexation in so short a time. It has, however, given us the satisfaction of coming before such an assembly as this, and if we live to be as old as our Illinois friend we may yet become eloquent, though it is written that "oppression makes a wise man mad."

Such unlawful and iniqutous doings have brought us into a lawsuit, which of all things we have been brought up to dread, and prefer to suffer much to avoid it. But could we do otherwise without giving up to mean cowardice by paying a "greedy neighbor the whole amount of tax and illegal costs to regain our meadow land, when we knew it was entirely contrary to law?" Though the case is appealed to the Hartford Court, it is thought it must be withdrawn, and if so, there will undoubtedly be an immediate raid upon all the movable articles in the house and on the premises. The law permits nothing to be exempt for taxes, though for debt it allows goods enough to keep house. But whatever is done to us we must bear it. After such unmerciful and lawless usage, I think none of our Suffrage friends in this assembly will advise us to falter, or to quietly advance the money and pay taxes. This we were

advised to do by a lawyer in Hartford, whom we had long consulted. Though he fully agreed that the law was on our side, he would commence no suit for redress. We cannot regret that it was taken up, for of all the iniquitous contrivances brought to light to deceive and cheat women, it surprised us the most.

The collector, in the return of his doings, asserted that after search, there could be no movable property found in his precincts. He saw no furniture, though sitting in our best furnished rooms, and had to confess, in answer to our able lawyer, that he looked not for wood in the woodhouse, nor for hay in the barn, nor did he even step over the way to inquire of the tenant whether there was stock on the farm, and he was expressly told that we owned the cows in the yard. Then all the items of the expenses were made out before the auction sale, many of them not accounted for at all. Our lawyer said such deeds might be lawful, but it was the custom not to make the charges till the work was done.

It was a trial worth hearing and seeing. The Glastonbury lawyer in his plea charged us with running down every man in town in order to render ourselves famous, but said that we should never live to see such a cause succeed, and much more he said not worth repeating. But we would not that this assembly should entertain the idea that we shall silently yield to taxation without representation, or hold our tongues when stringent laws are enforced, never enacted by the consent of the governed.

JULIA E. SMITH.

From the Woman's Journal, Nov. 14, 1874.

THE SISTERS SMITH AT TOWN MEETING.

EDITORS JOURNAL:— Perhaps, by this time, you may like a short notice of Glastonbury town affairs. The men here, laid another tax in September, the third on the list of 1873. The first $101 they collected from us by selling our cows at auction at an extra expense of $39. The second, of less than $50, they levied on our meadow land, selling eleven acres at an extra cost of $30; and apportioning it out among themselves beforehand. This being declared unlawful by the court, movable property coming first, they appealed to a higher court, intending, probably to let it lie there till they can get their deed recorded next June; of this last extra tax of about $150, due the first of November, the collector sent us the notice by mail.

A town meeting being called, on Monday of this week, to consider the expenses of the town, we attended, as it concerned us

4

more than anybody, the men intending to take more money from us than from anybody, as they had done for years past. We thought they might put us out of the house by force, as we should not go by request, having as good a right there as they had; and if they did, we should come back again, when we had a chance, unless they locked the doors. We came in when the meeting was opened, at ten A. M., and staid till it closed, at four P. M. Two men came up and talked with us at first, and one other in the course of the day. Our representative also, who voted for us in the Legislature last spring, came and spoke with us. He appears better than any of them, we think. The other representative is the collector, and constable also, who voted to have the whole matter of Woman's Rights dismissed at once. None of the authorities came near us. They have endorsed, 'tis said, the collector's doings, making us pay in that way more than anybody else in the town for having our meadow land unlawfully attached.

The men all seemed glad to see each other, but none smiled at seeing us, which is the last thing I believe they feel inclined to do. The meeting was conducted suitably enough for any woman to attend, but the house itself was very dirty. None of the men wore kid gloves but the lawyer who has counseled the town against us, so we took ours off. This lawyer occupies an office, owned by the man who has ruled the town for many years, but growing deaf, he patronized this one, putting him on the Republican side, that he might counsel both parties; and he joined the Congregational church, also.

The collector sat in a small place, parted off by itself, all the time nearly, in a corner of the room. He could not come out without facing us. The schools were the first business. It seems, the town employs nine men to visit the schools, at $3 a day, each having $6 apiece for examining four teachers, making a bill of $317. We have women here, who could have done the work more intelligently, all will say. One man, alone, does all the school business of Hartford, for $300.

The main business was to consider the expense of setting the boundary line between Glastonbury and Wethersfield. It was settled by the Legislature last spring, that the river was the boundary, at an expense of $5,000 for Glastonbury. We heard that our case was coming up under the head of expenses, but we were not mentioned. When the men stood before us so that we could not hear, we crowded up among them, without any outward action of disapproval.

We are now living in daily expectation of our furniture being seized, telling our friends we wish they would visit us while we have the use of it. We always thought we owned it, but find it belongs to the town, and we know not how long they will let it remain. We are not greatly enjoying this fine autum weather, but it is some comfort that the collector and his abettors are as much puzzled as we are, to know what is to be done with us next.

ABBY H. SMITH AND SISTER.
Glastonbury, Ct.

From the Woman's Journal, Feb. 13, 1875.

THE TRIAL OF THE SISTERS SMITH.

EDITORS WOMAN'S JOURNAL :—Again we have had the trial, during the past week, of passing through such a scene as has never been known in this land or in any other, so far as we have ever heard. Two women of our age, brought up in the dead of winter seven miles, by their own town, to stand before the State courts for three days to oppose the "principle," as the papers term their notices of it, of taxation without representation.

Our town not being willing to abide by the decision of one of their own justices, that when property is so taken, it must be taken according to the statute which says of all taxes expressly — that personal property must be taken first—the collector having sold land worth more than two thousand dollars for a tax of less than fifty dollars.

The question before the court was whether there was not any personal property to be found ? the collector having stated that, as a reason for levying on our land. When he called on us to demand the tax, he brought a man with him as a witness, it seems, to prove that we had no personal property worth the amount. He asked what we would turn out? and we replied we should not aid him in doing wrong—the furniture was before him, we thought we owned it, but found the town owned it and that he had the power to take what he pleased. The doors being open between the parlors, they were sitting where they could see both rooms. We had been advised, we said, to secrete our pictures, but we would not do it; we had always acted openly and fairly. We told him, too, there were our cows, we thought when Mr. Kellogg bid them off he could hold them, but our lawyer had told us that if they were driven back into our yard, we owned them as much as we ever did, and that they could be taken again as well. We asked him which he should take, the cows, or the furniture ? He said he thought he should take land this time.

On trial they both wholly denied all this,

or that we had told them one word about the cows. One of them testified that he would not have given the amount of the tax for all the furniture he saw. They went only into these two rooms, nor did they see if we had any other personal estate? Mrs. Kellogg happened to be present when they called, and testfying before we did, she stated clearly to the Court everything that was said upon the subject, and we confirmed it, being obliged to enumerate every article of furniture to prove (which we did) that in no place could a tax of that amount be more easily satisfied. It was clearly proved, also, that there was hay enough in the barn, corn enough in the cornhouse, and wood enough in the woodhouse, had he searched at all; which he acknowledged he had not done.

Their testimony about their doings in the meadow was of a piece with this. They had learned their part and all testified alike, four or five of them, differently from what they had testified before the Justice. It seemed to us we never had our feelings so tried in our lives as in their cross examinations; we thought we could not bear it, and my sister had to go out. We could not speak a word, though I did speak out twice, saying: "It was not so."

The trial lasted three days, the two first the longest we ever knew, the third day they made their pleas, and our lawyer Mr. Cornwall, brought them all out completely; so we think we cannot fail to get our case. The decision will not be brought in till the last of next week, for Mr. Cornwall raised some points of law as to the legality of the collector's warrant given him by the select men, which the Judge, whose behavior we liked, required some days to consider.

The collector had two lawyers, Judge Waldo and our town lawyer, Mr. Goslee, who accused us of greatly injuring the reputation of our town far and wide, and of making it a world of trouble. Judge Waldo attempted to prove that we owned no personal property (we have always been designated on the tax list as Hannah H. Smith's heirs, our mother owning the farm), and therefore that the collector must take land. Our counsel answered "Why then did he come to us for pay?" since our land is only assessed for one half of our taxes. He said we had done many worthy deeds and earned a good name, we had better have stopped there and not made the trouble we had made since, taking up the time, now, of the Court and of others so long; that the room was also much wanted for other cases and for the State, making so much additional expense, &c.

Mr. Cornwall replied that we ought by all means to resist an injury like this, and not to pay money where there was no law for it, we was not to blame for being brought to Hartford; our case had been decided before by a citizen of our own town.

The weather was very cold and bad; it rained hard one day. But we came home every night, for our two witnesses came with their horses, and we thought we would continue to sleep in our own house, while we have a house to sleep in.

Miss Ellen Burr has given the best account of our trial in the Hartford *Times* every day.

ABBY H. SMITH AND SISTER.
Glastonbury, Ct., Feb. 6, 1875.

From the Capital, Washington, D. C. Feb. 10, 1875.

SOUTH GLASTONBURY.

SOUTH GLASTONBURY, CT., February 10, 1875.

DEAR CAPITAL: When I first saw your paper I thought there was not another in the country in the least comparable to it for wit and wisdom, but now I have a suggestion to make, viz: That it would be well to slightly vary the weekly entertainment. It is understood that I wish to do this in the most respectful manner, as one should approach a king or an editor.

May I ask, then, why do you not notice the rest of the world outside of Washington and Baltimore, Glastonbury, for instance? Do you not know that here, just now, two women—Julia and Abby Smith—are fighting as good a battle for the chief principle of the Declaration of Independence as ever was fought in '76, and if you do know, do you care?

It is painfully interesting to read for the thousandth time that Miss Conna-Maria, O'Glorie-To-Hannah wore pink heavily corded silk to one reception, or that Mrs. Genora Superba Fishkettle wore point lace over heavy corded, spotless white silk, or that Mrs. Senator Thomas and Richard and Henry wore very heavy silks of yellow, pink and blue. We are glad, of course, that they can wear heavy, spotless silks and ape the manners of the aristocracy as well as they do, but, after the thousandth announcement of the wonderful fact, it ceases to call forth admiration or surprise.

Why, indeed, should it be surprising or interesting to read on one page that the drama of the "Forty Thieves" is being daily and hourly enacted in Washington, and to read on the next how a part of the wages are squandered by the wives and daughters of the actors? We are interested to know, not how many ounces of corded silks worn by the wives of Government officials weigh to the square inch, but whether the political rights of woman are much longer to be dependent upon the Government of such men as you so truthfully depict.

How would you like to be subjected to such a Government without a voice in the matter? How do you like to reflect that the fortune you may be able to leave to your daughters will not be so much theirs as it is that of every ignorant male voter, foreign or otherwise? When you consider how dependent man is, from the cradle to the grave, on woman's care and tenderness, can you not, being, as I am sure, sane gentlemen, say one word for her right of self-government, one word to save her from the hopelessness of her present condition.

Begging you to excuse me if I transgress, I am, most respectfully yours.

ROSELLA E. BUCKINGHAM.

IN MEMORIAM.

Died, at South Glastonbury, Conn., March 23, 1875, Mrs. ROSELLA E. BUCKINGHAM, aged 42. She was probably the most beautiful as well as the most talented woman ever reared in Glastonbury. She exerted herself in the cause of Woman Suffrage until her health gave out, and for nearly a year she was mostly confined to her bed by distressing illness. Her articles, published in the journals of the day, were powerful specimens of intellectual effort, and were inserted in many of the newspapers of Hartford, Springfield, Boston, Providence, Chicago, Washington, &c. The Suffrage cause has lost an able advocate and friend, and society one of its brightest ornaments.   J. E. S.

From the Woman's Journal, May 1, 1875

THE MELROSE CONVENTION.

Among the most effective incidents of the Convention were the appearance and speech of the sisters Smith of Glastonbury, Ct. These venerable ladies came together to the platform and spoke successively as follows:

ADDRESS OF ABBY H. SMITH.

We are much gratified to be among the number of our fellow citizens who have met this day to honor the deeds and principles of our forefathers, believing, as we do, that the honor consists wholly in practicing these principles, and not in making speeches, putting on uniforms, or firing guns. Our brethren who met at Concord two days ago, professedly for the same purpose that we have met, have taken into their hands all the legacies left by these, our common fathers, to their posterity, excluding their sisters from having any share in the advantages derived from their earnings and sufferings. These, our brothers, invited to partake with them in the festivities, their president, their governors, and all to whom they had given power to execute their laws — the authority of the land. And this very authority, who met at Concord to honor the great principles placed at the foundation of this republic, that "governments derive their just powers from the consent of the governed" and that "taxation without representation is tyranny," are now using their power to its utmost extent, to put down two lone women, well in years, from whom they have taken much money all their days, without allowing them any representation or remuneration even, and who are now standing without any help in the midst of the little conservative state of Connecticut, because these women have claimed their share in their common fathers' estate left to all their posterity, and from which they have never had the least benefit, being cast off by their brothers to earn their own living as best they might. And this they could have done, but their brothers, having more bodily strength, and being restricted by no law, would rob them continually, when money was wanted, and they could have no redress either by remonstrance or petition, for there were no laws made for their protection. This robbery being increased from year to year, as robbery always will be where there is no power to resist it, we could bear it no longer, and we did resist, though we knew that not only our property but our personal liberty was in their hands, to do with us as they pleased. Our resistance was the cause of the fight which has been going on ever since. They are determined to go to the extent of their laws and to take all we have, but we have never "consented" to these laws, and so they have no "just power" over us. But they pay not the least attention either to their own laws, or to their fathers' laws, however they may laud them in public. And these same men, the rulers over us, who met at Concord to honor our forefathers and their principles, are now sanctioning the holding of $2000 worth of our property, which they never helped to gain, but intend to keep, by changing their judges, so as to get those who will decide directly contrary to their own laws as printed on their statute books. They prevent our appealing to higher courts, having also threatened newspapers lest they should speak of us. And no wonder! Could this government glory and rejoice as they do in their foundation principles, giving liberty and equality to all the inhabitants of the land, if this case was known? Whatever has been done about us, has been contrived by a few beforehand in private.

And all this because we claim that we have as good a right to our forefathers' property as they have; we are as much the natural heirs. We have done as much to earn it as they have. Our money has gone as much for its defense and for its cultivation and improvements. Not only this, but our money has not been taken from our forefathers' estate, like theirs, but has been honestly earned, and has been forced from us without our having had any voice in the matter, or knowing what would be done with it, and without any remuneration; while they are paid for all they do on the property, taking much money for their work. Where this money comes from, let the pamphlet of William I. Bowditch answer.

ABBY H. SMITH.

ADDRESS OF JULIA E. SMITH.

JULIA E. SMITH at the Melrose meeting said:

These two women who have caused such a turmoil in their native place, and who have, their opponents say,—signally disgraced the ancient town of Glastonbury, Ct., now present themselves before you. It is quite agreeable to us to believe that our presence is desired in an audience of strangers whose faith is strong in the truth. What have we done? We have merely asserted that it is as wrong to take a woman's property without her consent, as it is to take a man's property without his consent; and we stand to it.

No man or woman denies this in conversation. For this we have had our pet cows seized and sold at the auction block, our whole meadow land attached, and eleven acres sold for a tax of not quite fifty dollars, worth more than two thousand dollars. For this unlawful deed we tried to get redress, and a prominent and upright citizen of our own town decided in our favor, according to the statute which expressly declares that real estate cannot be taken where personal estate can be found. But these unjust men appealed to the Hartford Court of Common Pleas, and brought us up for three days in the severity of winter, seven miles from our dwelling, and told us that Mr. Briscoe, the regular judge, was sick and we must be tried by George G. Sumner the City Judge. This was wholly false, for Judge Briscoe was hearing another case in the same building, and came in, the second day, and conversed with us. They must have a judge of the same politics as the town authority, who, it appears he did to others, had judged the case before it was heard. We have been told that he was in the lobby at the New Haven Legislature and was employed by Collector Andrews on the side of our town against Wethersfield, and two thousand dollars lobby money was spent to gain the case, which the town voted to pay, at the fall town meeting. It was called out by several members that they did not like to vote away the town's money without knowing how it was expended. A part of this expense comes upon the men. But thousands of dollars are yearly or oftener taken from women, without their knowing a word about it, or having the least voice in the matter. The judge took care to defer his decision two weeks and two days, so that it might be too late to bring the case be ore the court of errors for the March session, and then promised Mr. Cornwall, our lawyer, to give him the facts in the case. Our lawyer followed him from day to day, and can get nothing from him, for he says the papers are all lost and he remembers nothing about it. Our lawyer wrote down some of the facts, but he would not assent to them, for it seems to be the intention of the other side, to foil us entirely from bringing the case to the court of errors even so late as next fall. Mr. Cornwall has been obliged to sue the town, the collector, and Hardin who has a deed of the meadow land, to bring up the case before the Court of Equity to set aside the deed, and the Court has appointed a committee to take cognizance of the business. But Goslee the town lawyer objects to every one, and the Court will be obliged to appoint men of their own choice. The whole iniquity has been concocted beforehand, and their contrivance is, for our old enemy to record his deed before the year is up. Our lawyer seems to think that all this affair is so unlawful that there is no danger in letting it go over the year. But that we are not willing to suffer, for we cannot bear to see all our hay hauled up through our yard directly by the house for the advantage of such an ugly neighbor, and we do not see that it can aid the Suffrage cause to throw away, two or three thousand dollars, to our unspeakable injury. Did our forefathers pass through a seven years' bloody war, that only half their posterity should be benefited by the sacrifice? and be left without appeal either to town or state? The state took no notice of our petition (their being no discussion upon it) except to give us leave to withdraw; all the privilege we ever had from its laws. We seem to be left without a country, and we cannot see but we should fare better under a king; for King George himself never attached woman's property in so unfeeling and cowardly a manner as has been done to us. He merely tried to collect some duties of his subjects, and they had the privilege of refraining from drinking a cup of tea, which many of the women were brave enough to do a hundred years ago. Now men propose to celebrate their victory over taxation without representation by keeping a grand Centennial, while they leave half their citizens in a situation to suffer the same tyranny. We have now another tax hanging over our heads, of 150 dollars, sent us by mail last October, which they do not at present venture to collect, as has been intimated to us, until the next session of the Legislature, when they will get an *ex post facto* law passed, as they have done before, to sanction their illegal doings. It may therefore be possible we shall have a furnished house to receive our friends in, till next June.

These two solitary women, who have not a relative to defend them, seem to stand on so firm a foundation that it requires, to put them down, a whole State and all the authority of a town, who break their own laws, silence the newspapers from speaking of them, change the regular court judge, and no doubt will pass new State laws against them; yet have they not succeeded in moving them from their stronghold.

JULIA E. SMITH.

Glastonbury, Ct.

From the Hartford Daily Post.

THE GLASTONBURY COWS.

To the Editors of the Evening Post:

SIR: I have noticed a paragraph in your paper apparently from your Glastonbury correspondence, which says that the attorney of the Misses Smith has appeared in town and settled for them the taxes they so stoutly resisted. This is not true; so far as their attorney is concerned I have never paid any tax for them to the town of Glastonbury, their collector or any one else, and the matter relating to the claimed unjust proceeding against these ladies is not settled, but still in court, and is, and will be resisted until the questions involved are, if need be, passed upon by our supreme court. On the 15th of the present month two other parties in Glastonbury were sued by the Misses Smith for the unlawful part they took in the matter of enforcing their taxes against them, which suit will be tried before Justice Hollister on the 3d of July, unless for cause the same shall be postponed.

These ladies as well as other citizens of this state, desire to know if the law be so that $2,500 worth of their estate can be seized and disposed of without redress for an unlawful tax of $49, and they have a right to know.

Yours respectfully,

H. CORNWALL.

From the Woman's Journal, June 26, 1875.

NO JUSTICE FOR CONNECTICUT WOMEN.

EDITORS JOURNAL.—We have paid our tax at the point of the bayonet. When you fall into the hands of banditti and have turned every way and done all in your power to escape and find no escape for you, you must yield to their demands. Our case is so perfectly parallel to the account given in the Bible of Naboth the Jezreelite, taking the literal meaning, that we can think of nothing else.

Our adversaries set up a judge of their own, removing the regular one, and substituting in his stead, another whom they had reason to think would decide as they wished to have him. They then testified before him, under oath, in face of all the people who could see and know to the contrary, that they could not find on our precincts enough personal property to satisfy the tax, and had therefore levied on our land. This was the whole question.

And then Hardin, who held the deed against us, swore that he bid for the land on the premises when no bidding was done there; for we stood by the collector the whole time, and he told us when he first came that the land was already bargained for. Hardin was seen on the public street in front of his house before 2 o'clock, the time set for the sale, talking earnestly with the collector, and he continued there till 3, while we were waiting in the meadow for them. He then came into court and swore, supported by the collector, that they had said nothing about the sale beforehand, when no other bidder was there, and the three surveyors, all of them persons of their party on the land, confirmed what they said.

The collector, Andrews, testified in court that Hardin would not take less land than he measured off for him. When did they make their agreement, not being seen to talk together on the lot, where they staid not more than twenty minutes or half an hour. There were five of their party, and five of ours, and Andrews told us, when he first came on, how much he should measure off for the tax. How came he to know how much he should measure off beforehand?

While they were doing this, Hardin came up to our party and said he wanted nothing to do with the business, and we said it was all unlawful.

"Well, it makes no difference with me," he replied, " I am indemnified; I shall lose nothing by it." When was he indemnified, if not beforehand? This sham trial, which lasted three days, was undertaken wholly to put us off without any hearing till after the 20th of June, when they knew that if we could not get any, we must pay, though they knew, also, as well as we did, that there was no law in their case whatever. But, as they have the Legislature, with the whole state, as well as the town, on their side, none of them regarding laws where politics rule, we dare not venture the result, having all the available part of our farm at stake.

The judge in our case witheld his decision for two weeks and two days, till the time was past when we could appeal to the March court, and then decided against us, without giving any reason for it whatever, and our lawyer can get none, after the most persevering and continued application to him; for we must give some reason to a higher court for appealing to them from the decision of a lower one.

The Judge says that the papers are lost, and all we can get from him in writing is that, "in the opinion of the collector, there was no personal property to be found."

Our lawyer has done all in his power to get a hearing somewhere. He has sued the officers of the town to bring them before a court of equity, and many promises are made to him which are never intended to be kept. But where everything is under a ruling power, which regards nothing but votes, neither promises nor laws can be depended on. Our lawyer is determined not to give it up, and says he never will, till he can get some justice done. He is contriving to go on with the business, and we are very glad to have him do so. What the official's will do with their 150 dollar tax, so unlawfully assessed and sent to us by mail last October, we cannot now tell. But we suppose they are waiting for the Legislature to pass the "General Healing Act," which they have sent in to them, so that the officers of the town may do as they desire to do with us and our property, without being called to any account for it.

Did England do anything to our forefathers in the way of taxation without representation, iniquitous as this?

ABBY H. SMITH AND SISTER.
Glastonbury, Ct.

From the Hartford Daily Times, July 9, 1875.

Miss Julia Smith addressed the committee after Gen. Lee finished his argument. The committee and the audience all drew about her and listened with great interest. She wanted to tell the committee about a "General Healing Act," which had been introduced into the present legislature from Glastonbury, to make legal some illegal doings of officers in that town. These doings related solely to the Misses Smith, and the speaker said she didn't know that they were of sufficient importance, especially at their time of life, to have the legislature pass an act referring exclusively to them. She thought if anybody needed a "healing act," it was she and her sister, for their rights and their feelings had been sufficiently disturbed to require healing. [Great cheering and applause from the audience.] She said they had been told that they had the right of petition, and so they did petition the legislature, and the legislature gave them leave to withdraw. This touch of sarcasm brought down the house again. She spoke of the large amount they had paid in taxes to the town of Glastonbury—larger than any other person in the town—and yet, when she and her sister went to the town house to address the people assembled there, they refused them; but the people on the outside said they should be heard, and assisted them into a cart. "Yes," said the speaker, "we find we have some rights; we can speak from a cart; and we are allowed to withdraw our petition from the legislature." The committee asked them a good many questions, for Miss Abby Smith spoke before the hearing was over, and some of the committee proposed that they go down to the Smith farm, and view the movable property of the sisters; and also the land illegally seized by the collector. It was acknowledged by many who listened to Miss Smith's statement that the seizure was illegal, and the decision of the court last February, unjust, as all Glastonbury, including the collector, knew they had plenty of movable property. In fact, when the collector called, they pointed out their cows to him and told him he could take their furniture if he wished.

From the Woman's Journal. July 10, 1875.

VISIT TO THE SISTERS SMITH.

"What is so rare as a day in June?"

Nothing except the early days of July. So I thought when, on the first day of this month, we went from Boston to Hartford, to see if anything could be done to induce the Connecticut Legislature to pass a law to enable women to vote for President and Vice-President of the United States, as they are fully empowered to do by the National Constitution.

It was one of the days. The deep blue of the sky looked down through great masses of white cumulus clouds, whose shadows flitted over the waving grass. The rivers were all "green rivers," made so by the abundant foliage on their margins. The ponds, without a ripple, reflected sky, clouds, trees and shrubs, till the beauty and the stillness made one almost forget even the political and legal injustice done to women.

The Legislative Committee gave a respectful hearing. At the conclusion of it, the sisters Smith were ready with two carriages, to take us over the seven miles which lie between Hartford and Glastonbury. The road the whole distance is shaded by maple and elm trees, whole rows of which were planted, nearly a hundred years ago, by French refugees, the good soldiers of Lafayette. To-day they stand with their almost century of growth, shading the road over which the cows of the sisters Smith were driven to be sold, and up and down which they themselves go, in their peaceful effort to secure the same rights for which Lafayette left France, and for which the war of the Revolution was made.

This house, which will be forever historic, is a large two story house, painted white, with green shutters. It is shaded by fine old elms, under which in the dooryard a meeting of Garrisonian abolitionists was held many years ago, when no other place could be had in the town for it.

Here live the sisters, who are as truly defending the principle of representative government as were the men who fought and died at Bunker Hill.

Behind the house are the eleven beautiful acres, which the collector seized for a tax of less than fifty dollars, and there, too, feed the famous cows, for the present safe with their rightful owners.

The neighbors of the sisters show genuine sympathy with them in their contest with the successors of Geo. III, who mean to compel them to pay taxes while they are denied representation.

It did one's heart good to see the couragous, honest little woman, who refused to touch a drop of the milk of the cows, while they were held in custody on her premises, previous to the sale.

It renewed one's faith in human integrity to hear Mrs. K. reiterate her testimony before the court, while her face, better than any oath, proved the truth of every word she said.

But, best of all is the faith, courage and determination of the sisters themselves. The State of Connecticut, loud for the Centennial, is against them. The Legislature gave them leave to withdraw their petition for equal rights. Still they prosecute their claim for justice, from court to court, sure that each rising sun brings them nearer to the triumph of the principle they are seeking to establish. They say they mean to hold the law-makers to their own laws.

By the law of Connecticut, personal property must always be taken for taxes, before real estate is levied on. But the collector sat in a room, where was a full length gilt framed mirror, which alone is worth more than the amount of the tax; there are good Brussels carpets on all the floors below, and pictures whose frames would cost more than a hundred dollars. The rooms are full of furniture, but the collector swore that he did not see personal property worth fifty dollars in the house. He, accordingly, advertised their best meadow, to satisfy the tax. The sisters, with Mr. and Mrs. K., were early on the ground on the day of sale; too early. But as the collector did not make his appearance, they thought that may be they were at the wrong place and so started to look for the officers of the law. When they had proceeded a little distance, they saw the collector coming to the place they had left. They returned at once, and were told that the land was sold. They heard no bid, nor any call for a bid.

This is only a specimen of the illegal and unjust treatment they have received. But they are sure they are right, and so loose neither heart nor hope.

They go over the long road heavy with sand, to Hartford, to attend the court, and then back to the honest freedom of their simple hospitable home, where Miss Julia reads Greek as easily as other women do English, and where Miss Abby amuses herself with the beautiful flowers around the house, and with pleasant interchange of opinion with her friendly neighbors.

As I went through the rooms where these brave women live, it seemed to me that the spot whereon I stood was holy ground. Here began a peaceful resistance to the same kind of tyranny as that which caused the war of the Revolution; and here, some day, as to Bunker Hill now, will come men and women who are reverent of the great principle of the consent of the governed, who respect courage and fidelity to principle, and who will hold at its true value, the part which these sisters have taken in solving the meaning of a representative government.

Since writing the above, we learn by a private letter from the sisters, that on Saturday last, both parties appeared before Justice Hollister, who decided for the sisters, awarding them $100 and costs. The case was appealed to the September Court.

                            LUCY STONE.

From the People, August 15, 1875.

INTERESTING CORRESPONDENCE.

Editor of THE PEOPLE :—

Your readers have heard of Abby and

Julia Smith, of Glastonbury; the women who believe that "Taxation and Representation" should go hand-in-hand, and who suffered the sale of their property—to the amount of two thousand of dollars—in preference to submitting to be taxed where they could not be represented. It seems that they are scholars, as well as patriots; as the following interesting and valuable correspondence will show. These letters are addressed to a gentleman in this city:

GLASTONBURY, CT., July 20, '75.

———— ———— Dear Sir; My sister and I would like your advice. We are all that are left of five unmarried sisters living together in the old homestead, till death parted us. In the time of the Miller excitement we became much interested in a near friend—making six of us—to learn the exact meaning of every word of the original language by which God had spoken to us. We think there are three inspired versions, Hebrew, Greek, and Latin, those over the head of our Saviour, by which God has spoken to us. The sister who is now left with me, had studied the Greek testament after finishing her Latin at school, and she now began setting down the English of every Greek word, without regarding the sense, and also one meaning, instead of different meanings, to the same Greek word, as our translators have often done. She then procured a Septuagint Bible, and translated that in the same way. By the advice of a very learned friend she studied Hebrew, to find the meaning of the names, and translated the whole of that Bible, as she had done the others. She then translated the Latin Vulgate, and afterward, 'or her own amusement, she wrote, again, the Bible all out from the Greek and Hebrew; making five times she has written that book throughout, with her own hands.

She had never intended publishing these translations, till our town had persecuted us so unjustly about our taxes, selling off more than two thousand dollars worth of our land for a tax of less than fifty dollars. This was expressly contrary to the statute, which requires all movable property to be taken first; but being backed by the authority of the whole State, we could get no hearing in any court, and were obliged to yield.

We thought it might help our cause to have it known that a woman could do more than any man has ever done, while we are denied all protection from any quarter, made to pay more money than any of the inhabitants of the place, without any voice in the matter. No country owns us — robbed by all.

We rode over to Hartford, yesterday, and called at several houses to learn the cost of publication. Shall learn definitely, tomorrow, the actual cost from one of the best houses. But t it occurred to us, this morning that perhaps you would know if it could be done with less expense in Philadelphia. Will you answer this soon, and tell us your opinion of the whole matter. There would be no marginal readings, and no words supplied. It is merely the English word for the original text. If there is anything to be made by publishing this work, we would like it to be made by *suffragists*. We do not expect in our life-time to realize enough from the sale of the books to pay the cost of publication. We should publish one thousand copies, at first as soon as could be done.

Yours, very respectfully,

ABBY AND JULIA SMITH.

The gentleman, in replying, asked, whether they would not the better subserve the cause for which they had suffered and sacrificed so much, by using the money that the book would cost in advocating directly the doctrine that "Taxation and Representation" can not be rightly separated and received the following reply, dated August 1, 1875:

We received your letter in due time. Having requested you to give us your opinion of the whole matter, we expected you would give it to us, of course.

You think the money we should expend for our publication would help the suffrage cause more than the publication would. We have little faith in money to help us at all. It never helped the temperance cause, in which we used to labor; and every church in the land is founded on it—while God's truth comes to all *who thirst for it*, "without money, and without price." God governs the world by moral means; and no logic can be plainer, no truth can be clearer, than, if it be wrong to take a man's property without his consent, must be equally wrong to take a woman's property without her consent; and the men, therefore, must take it from her on the ground that her intellect is not as strong as theirs; the women are not as capable of going into all kinds of knowledge as the men are, (and which is required of men to govern;) that men are able to search deeper into every kind of learning. Now there is no learning that is so much respected by the whole world—let their religious belief be what it may—as the knowledge of the most ancient languages, in which the Bible was written—the three over the head of our Saviour. They must have been given by God; for the instruction of all three are so perfect they could not, possibly, be altered; and they are now dead languages, and can never be changed, by speaking, as modern languages are. And here is a woman, with no motive but the love of doing it, and no instructions since her school-days, has gone further, alone, in translating these languages, than any man has ever gone, and without any of his help, *and no law of the land gives her any protection.* The men where she lives can take as much as they please of her property, and she can have no voice in the matter, nor any redress from any quarter. If this be not robbery, there is no such thing as robbery; but if those who uphold this robbing find that those they rob know more than they do, it must have weight with them. It is knowledge that rules the world.

We have been greatly encouraged, this summer. We had not intended to address the legislative committee again; for last year they gave us "leave to withdraw our petition," which was, praying to be be put on an equality with the other citizens of the State, without ever considering it at all, that we could ever learn. But this year we spoke before the committee, upon the spur of the moment, the last of the speakers telling them our whole story, and we have never seen men appear more interested. They gathered around us, asking us the very questions we liked to answer, and brought in a unanimous report in favor of the petition, which was, for woman-suffrage at the next presidential election, and, out of 189 who voted on the question, 82 were in our favor. This must have been a great blow to the State, without whose help our town could never have done as they did to us; and no paper is allowed to print a word upon the subject, for fear of hurting the Centennial, we suppose.

It seems our State has given twenty-five thousand dollars to your Centennial, to glorify principles which neither the men who got it up, or our forefathers, ever practiced, or ever intended to practice; neither do those who vote this money: but they may be obliged to, for truth ever comes up at the last. It is never suppressed. The legislature also gave $1,000,000 for a new State-house for the use of half the citizens, intending to make the other half pay as much for it as if they could use it.

We learned, last week, there was a publishing-house in Hartford that favored our cause, and will assist us in selling our books. We have never expected the sale of the books would pay the expense of publishing, which will be about five thousand dollars. We can spare this money, and we propose, also, selling off half our land, [owning one hundred and thirty acres, from half of which we derive no profit,] that our town may not be able to take more from our property than from any of its citizens, as it has done heretofore.

They have gone contrary to their own laws in their proceedings against us, and in the fall, when the trials come on, may have the "cost to pay,"—and we may have it to pay; but nothing can move us from the firm foundation on which we stand. We should like to hear from you whenever you can find time to write.

ABBY H. SMITH AND SISTER.

From the Windham County Transcript, Aug. 19, 1875.

LETTER FROM HARTFORD,

BY A LADY JOURNALIST.

Hartford, Aug. 14th, 1875.

EDITOR TRANSCRIPT:—It is said that everybody in Connecticut has heard the story of Abby Smith and her cows; but possibly some may have forgotten it, and it is barely possible, too, that some may not have heard of it; so I am led, Mr. Editor, to rehearse the story in brief; the more so, as I am told the Smith sisters are to be present at a public entertainment in your vicinity before long,—at a festival in the Congregational church at Dayville, on the evening of the 27th inst.

Though Miss Julia, the older of the two sisters, is the one who raised the cows, Miss Abby is the one who raised the breeze, and made herself famous and the cows too. But Miss Julia is likely to be quite as well known to the world in the future, for she built her own monument, and laid the foundation of an enduring fame some 25 years ago, when she translated from the Hebrew, the whole Bible; and so anxious was she to get a literal translation, that she went through the whole work a second time; and then made two translations from the Greek, and one from the Latin. Five translations of the entire Bible! an immense labor all must acknowledge, and one never accomplished by any one man. Indeed, I am not aware that any man ever made one entire translation of the whole Bible from the Hebrew unaided. Wicklif's the first complete translation, into English, was not from Hebrew, but from the Latin. John De-Tervisa, cotemporary with Wicklif, made a complete translation, but his, also, was from the Vulgate. Tyndale's translation which, after so many revisions, forms our present common translation, was not the whole of it the work of Tyndale. He translated the whole of the New Testament, and the Old to the end of the Second Book of Chronicles, making just two-thirds the entire Scriptures, and here his labor ended by the papal persecution which committed him to the flames, and the translation completed by his friend Thomas Matthew, or more generally known as John Rogers, the martyr at the stake in the days of "bloody Mary." After many revisions at different hands, this translation received its final and most elaborate one, at the hands of the celebrated 47 translators under King James, which is the translation we are all familiar with. The Bible has been worked up by many different hands, and has appeared under different names, as "Wiclif's Bible," "Tyndale's Bible," "Coverdale's Bible," "Cranmer's Bible," and "King James's Bible," but I cannot find that any one man over made a complete translation from the Hebrew, much less, five complete translations of the Bible. This was left to a woman to do; an unpretending, unassuming little woman, who modestly shut the work up in her closet for a quarter of a century, intending to die with it there, had not the urgency of others brought it out. And now she is making preparations to publish it in this city. It will probably be issued from the press some time next spring. What would the old monkish doctor, Henry deKnyghton have said to this? Here is what he said of Wiclif's translation—for he was cotemporary with him: "This Master John Wiclif hath translated the gospel out of Latin into English, which Christ had intrusted with the *clergy and doctors* of the church that *they* might minister it to the laity and weaker sort, according to the state of the times and the wants of the men. So that by this means the gospel is made vulgar, and more open to the laity, and even to women who can read, than it used to be to the most learned of the clergy and those of the best understanding!"

Poor old monk! I'm afraid Julia Smith would have set his old head buzzing if he had lived in these degenerate days; to say nothing of Abby and her cows. But where are they? Completely overshadowed, I'm afraid, by the weightier matters that lie between the lids of a Bible, or rather, which lie at present in the modest manuscript. But I must go back once more to my subject,—for I'm rather enchanted with it myself—and tell you that I've been allowed a peep at this manuscript. And I will give you what struck me as a happy rendering of old time wisdom. Our common translation says: "Now when Jesus was born in Bethlehem of Judea in the days of Herod the king, behold, there came wise men from the east to Jerusalem." Julia Smith's translation says: "Now when Jesus was born in Bethlehem of Judea in the days of Herod the king, behold there came wise men from the sunrisings to Jerusalem."

Miss Smith claims her translation to be absolutely literal. But others have claimed the same thing. Different scholars have, in certain cases, given a different translation to the same word, from the fact that all do not see alike. Thus King James's translators have put the word "charity," where Tyndale used the word "love," and "church," where he used "congregation." Many critics have pronounced Tyndale's translation the better of the two. Tyndale also claims a literal interpretation; and in his reply to Chancellor More, he says: "I call God to record against the day we shall appear before our Lord Jesus, to give a reckoning of our doings, that I never altered one syllable of God's Word, against my conscience." Julia Smith claims the same, an absolutely literal rendering. And scholars and critics will, doubtless, be glad to get hold of this work,—some for the purpose of picking it to pieces, because it is the work of a woman; and others, for the sake of seeing what a woman can do in this line; and others, for the sake of comparing notes, because it is a new translation, which, in itself, is not a small event; and lastly—though perhaps I should have put them firstly,—those who believe a woman has as good a brain as a man, and can turn out as good work; therefore, they will glory in possessing this Bible.

But I have more than filled my space, and Abby Smith and the Alderneys are left in the lurch. But that touches another chapter, so entirely foreign to this one that I have inadvertently and almost unconsciously branched out upon, that I shall have to leave it, for the present at least, hoping that those of you who wish to pick up the thread I have dropped, will do so by the assistance of Miss Abby herself, whom they will find at the festival alluded to, or at Mrs. Dr. Hammond's in Dayville, where the sisters are to visit a day or two at that time. They know nothing about this mention I make of them, but I know there are many good people in your vicinity, who would be glad to see the Misses Smith, and so I have ventured to inform them of their opportunity.   F. E. B.

From the Woman's Journal, Aug. 23, 1873.

THE GLASTONBURY CONTEST.

EDITORS WOMAN'S JOURNAL.—After an interval of a year and four months, during which time our town authorities have never called on us, the Collector came to see us yesterday. We asked him, at once, if he had come to take our property. He said he hoped we should pay him some money now. We told him it was as just and right for us to go his house and demand his money, as it was for him to come to our house to get our money. It appeared to us the strangest thing in the world that after living here all our lives, well known to everybody, and paying the town so much money as we had, that the town should be willing to have us treated in the way we had been—selling off two thousand dollars worth of our property to pay a tax of less than fifty dollars.

"And we could have taken all you had," said he, "if none had bid less."

"And here you stood," we replied, "in front of Hardin's house, he the only bidder, in earnest talk for a whole hour, while we were waiting in the meadow, and then both of you came into court and swore that you had said nothing about the business beforehand. When did you make all the agreements spoken of after you came on the ground? And then you and Mr. Brainard testified under oath that there was not property enough in these rooms to satisfy a tax of fifty dollars."

"Well," he said, "it was a bad thing to take furniture; you are obliged to move and store it, and then perhaps you could not sell it."

We had a lady with us from New Haven, the very one we would have chosen, who could join with us and remember all that was said. We told him we never knew before that a judge could be changed, but in our case it was necessary to have one with whom they had lobbied in the Legislature in New Haven, and knew of course that he would decide as they wanted him to.

He declared that it was not our case that his business had been about in New Haven; it was the Wethersfield line.

We told him we knew that, and they knew that if he would do what he did for them in that line, costing our town two thousand dollars, he was the one to do the business for them in this case.

He said that the judge was changed because the regular judge was sick, and that his wife, too, was very sick and died.

We told him that his wife attended the court the first day, and lived for several weeks after, and that the judge himself the same day was trying another case in the building our court was held in, and came to see us at noon—facts not to be denied. We added that nothing could be more unjust than to come and take our property from us whenever they chose, without our having any advantage from it.

He said we had protection and the use of the roads.

We asked what kind of protection it was, when we could be robbed with impunity at any time; and when, although our money went for the roads, we could have no voice in regard to them?

We could not find out what he intended to do with us. We thought it probable that as our lawyer had gone to Saratoga to stay till the first of September, they intended to do something with us meanwhile. It was

the tax of one hundred and fifty dollars which they sent us by mail last October, that he wanted us now to pay. The collector said that there was a drain tax due of three dollars, for a drain, that divides the meadow from the upland. This we paid last year, because in regard to this we could vote like the other proprietors, and we paid him that tax cheerfully, for we had attended those meetings and voted, several years ago, greatly to our satisfaction.

ABBY H. SMITH AND SISTER.
Glastonbury, Ct.

From the Windham County Transcript,
Sept. 2, 1875.

REPORT OF A FAIR AND FESTIVAL,
HELD IN DAYVILLE, (KILLINGLY) AUG.
27, 1875.

After this piece, Misses Abby and Julia Smith of Glastonbury, Conn., were escorted to the platform and introduced to the audience. Standing side by side, Miss Julia Smith, in a happy, off-hand style, spoke of their native town, making a few humorous and sarcastic hits, and drawing applause from an interested audience. Her sister, Miss Abby Smith, next read this earnest plea.

"Is there any truth on earth clearer to the comprehension of everybody—to our natural common sense,—to all the ideas we imbibe from our childhood, —to say nothing about law or religion than what is wrong to do to a man is equally wrong to do to a woman? If this be not logic, there is no such thing as logic. There is no such thing as truth on earth, if this be not truth, that commends itself to every man's conscience — that every man knows to be right. If this be not so, there can be no religion; for if woman must look to man to guide her before she looks to God, why, she looks to a being equally sinful as herself, to whom God has directed all his threatenings if he does not repent. Does man plead that woman is not included in these threatenings (which must be the natural consequence of his superority) the same as himself? Why then does he preach to him? Has God made him more holy? Neither nature nor our religion prove this. Does he ever try to show that these threatenings are directed to her more than to him as the most guilty? On what ground then does he attempt to prove that he should be more favored than she, that he should have greater privileges before the law? He must plead animal strength; there is no other reason for it under heaven but that. Man forgets how he was created in the beginning. It is written "God created man in his image, in the image of God created he him; male and female created he them. And God blessed them and said unto them, 'Be fruitful and multiply and replenish the earth and subdue it; and have dominion over the fish of the sea, and over the fowl of the air, and over every living thing that moveth upon the earth.'" Did God make any distinction between the male and the female? And how do we rule over these animals? Not by greater physical strength, for theirs is sometimes more than ours, but by our greater intellect which God has given us to rule over a kind lower than ourselves. Does God give us the least intimation, throughout his whole word, that he has given more intellect to the man than to the woman? It could not possibly be, because one is born of the other, and, in consequence, must have the same intellect. We see he has made no difference in that respect in any of the animals; they govern each other merely by physical strength. Shall man copy from them and rule as he now does, in the same way, making woman of the brute creation? not seeing that in the same way that he darkens her intellect and makes her his slave he darkens his own. To perpetuate slavery man has always been obliged to take away knowledge from the slave, and bring him down as near an animal as possible. Look at all the heathen in the world worshipping idols and even animals. Is not this the way they have been brought so low, by taking away all intellect from their women till they have none left themselves? 'Tis surely the natural consequence Children, take after their mother the same as from their father, and more, for the mother has the care of them in childhood. England could conquer India tho' thousand of miles away, because knowledge was brought over in her ships. In this way the Indians of our land have been and are now conquered. The white man knows the most. The Indian cannot possibly conquer, born and brought up by such wives as he makes to serve him. 'Tis the same in China and India. Instead of rising, they must sink lower and lower until their women can be put on an equality with the men. In vain you send them missionaries. One hundred years ago our nation began to rise, and she did rise, for she inscribed on her banners Liberty and Equality; and people from all parts of the earth flocked to her for protection. She declared her foundation principle to be, "Governments derived their just power from the consent of the governed," and yet she has tried hard, ever since, to govern with the consent of but half the people, the other half receiving no benefit whatever from her laws, and are obliged to support them as much as those who do receive benefit. Her other great foundation principle is, that "Taxation without representation is tyranny," and she has never ceased to carry out this principle against the helpless—against those who could not resist, since she became a government, putting these helpless ones into the hands of the ignorant officers of the towns where they live, to take their property from them whenever they please, and as much as they please, and from whose exactness there is no redress—no appeal to a higher power. They have no country to protect them. Better far for them to have remained under England; far better for them had this glorious revolution, so called, never been achieved. None of its benefits have ever descended to them. They are still taxed without representation and governed without their consent.

After the exercises in the church, the company repaired to the lecture room below where the guests and many others partook of good things cooked and eaten in dishes a hundred years old.

From the Woman's Journal. Nov. 6, 1875.

THE BIBLE TRANSLATION OF JULIA E. SMITH.

The following letter was received in answer to an enquiry as to whether it was true that the translation by Miss Julia E. Smith was to be published;

DEAR MRS. STONE:—. . . . My sister Abby has a strong desire to have it done. To be sure, we both know, there is no reason under heaven why women cannot control their own property, only that they do not know as much as men. Printing a translation from the original tongues would show that one woman has done, without aid, what one man has never done; and this woman is not considered by the men capable of managing what she rightfully and lawfully owns, as the Collector said the other day he could take all she had. I have written out the Bible five times, twice from the Greek, twice from the Hebrew, and once from the Latin. These three were written over the head of our Saviour, and are dead languages, and cannot be altered, the construction is so perfect.

Some twenty years ago, we five sisters, with one friend, had a strong desire to know the literal meaning of many texts we had examined together. The Latin and Greek I studied when a school girl, and first translated the Greek New Testament, then the Septuagint, and, from the suggestion of a learned friend, I got a knowledge of the Hebrew in order to learn the meaning of the proper names. I wrote it out word for word generally putting the same English word for the same Greek and Hebrew word, not giving my own sense of it, but letting it speak for itself, without addition or subtraction. Next I translated the Roman Bible, the Vulgate. It never once entered my mind, at that time, that it could be published, but we all thought my way of giving the meaning made an easier understanding of the text. We have another inducement to publish. We think we have money enough in Hartford banks to pay the expense of the work, which will relieve the town of half our taxes, as the bank stock is assessed as much as the farm; and we may sell off yet a part of that, and not be obliged to pay more money than anybody else. One of the publishing houses told us that they thought they might sell enough to indemnify us for the expense; but that we do not expect, and we do not see that spending our money in this way will injure anybody. We are waiting to hear from the American Publishing Company to tell us how much they estimate the expense.

Yours sincerely,
JULIA AND ABBY SMITH.

Since the above was received the Sisters Smith have contracted with the American Publishing Company, in Hartford, to print their translation of the Bible, and it is now going through the press. **L. S.**

From the Springfield Union, Nov. 27, 1875.

THE SMITH BIBLE.

NOTE FROM MISS JULIA E. SMITH.

To the Editor of The Union:

I was much pleased to see in your issue of last Saturday's Daily UNION a notice of my translation of the Hebrew Bible, now in the hands of the American Publishing Company at Hartford. Nor am I the least surprised that you should say that "Miss Smith's publication of a private translation is an amazing exhibition of conceit." Especially "in view of the fact that a translation of the Bible is about the most difficult task that the most erudite scholars can set themselves, and is at present monopolizing the labors of an international association of the most eminent biblical critics in the world." No wonder it should be thought that an ordinary woman, brought up on a farm, with no particuliar advantages of literary society, must have an extraordinary portion of self confidence to put in print a translation of an inspired work, without going to the learned for help. This translation was never made for the public, but for the gratifieation of six persons, the five sisters Smith and one friend. They were all much interested, some twenty or thirty years ago, in searching the Scriptures after the notorious Miller doctrine came out, and they met weekly for that purpose. They were all anxious to know the literal meaning of every word God had spoken, and as I had got a knowledge at our academy when a school girl, of Greek and Latin, I began the translation of the Greek New Testament. As I put the same English word for the same word in Greek, it gave a much clearer view of the text. I then rendered the Septuagint into English, at the advice of a most learned friend, who said the Hebrew was a very simple language, easily learned, as there was but one book of pure Hebrew in the world, and that was the Bible. He also wrote that if I would learn that tongue I could see with my own eyes, and not through the glasses of my neighbors. I followed his advice and a most delightful work it was, making the whole agree, taking the New Testament with it, from Geneses to Revelation. I was sufficiently paid and wrote out the Greek and Hebrew twice each, and the Vatican Bible, the Vulgate, once. I cannot be afraid of criticism, for let any one get a thorough knowledge of any language, especially one of such a perfect grammatical construction, and let it be rendered literally word for word, without the consideration of the opinion of the writer, how can any person get aside? They show no theological preference, but let the book testify for itself, without addition or subtraction. The marginal readings and the words in italics in our English translation show that King James's forty-seven translators were not exactly satisfied. I have let the Hebrew make sense for itself, without going according to my own ideas of the meaning. These three ancient languages, Latin, Greek, and Hebrew, were put over the head of our Saviour; they are dead languages and cannot be altered. The grammar of no spoken language is so complete.

Never had it entered our minds that this work could come before the public until last Summer, when our meadow land was illegally sold by the town authority. They must have gone upon the supposition that they were capable of taking care of what belonged to women than were the women themselves. The collector said the last time that he called that he had a right to take all we had if he pleased. And they do take when they please, and as much as they please. We wanted them to understand that the woman who knew not enough to manage what she rightfully and lawfully owned had actually done what no man ever had. Not that she was more capable of voting for that, for I consider that every citizen who has common sense and common education, and of a reputable character, is entitled to a vote, one as much as another. Never have I considered myself above others for having translated the Bible. Still I think we ought to be respected enough for men not to break their own laws to get possession of our property. We certainly have not broken their laws though we are not bound to keep them, "for goverments derive their just powers from the consent of the governed," and we have by no means ever consented to be governed in this way. We did not expect indemnity for the expense of printing the Bible, but felt that it was some satisfaction to take our stock from the Hartford banks, which is assessed about as much as the farm, and it would relieve us of half our taxes. Should not a volume be sold, we have a perfect right to spend our money as we please, as we pay for the work and injure nobody. We have not a relative in the world near enough to claim anything of ours or say, Why do you do so.

We have now Thanksgiving day to ourselves, and do feel thankful that we have been noticed enough for us to say a few words in your paper. Last year at this time one of the Hartford papers said that the Misses Smith of Glastonbury had declared they would never eat another Thanksgiving supper till they could vote, and they thought we must go without that fare for some time. We did say that we did not feel thankful enough after such usage to cook anything for Thanksgiving or even eat it in this town, and we continue to feel so. Therefore, this day I have had the satisfaction of giving you some explanation about the self confidence I have shown in bringing out my Bible. Yours respectfully,
JULIA E. SMITH.
Glastonbury, Ct., November 25, 1875.

From the Hartford Daily Times, Dec.
11, 1875.

AN ORIGINAL FAMILY.

The "Smith sisters," of Glastonbury, who have waked up, not in youth, but in the fullness of years, to find themselves famous, are remarkable for something more than their celebrated Alderney cows and their zeal for female suffrage. This action of theirs, in letting the town authorities levy on, take and sell their favorite cows for taxes which they would not pay, for the alleged reason that they, being women, had had no part nor lot in making the tax laws, was one of many traits of their marked character. It is true they got their cows back again, and probably received, in admiring contributions from various parts of the country (thanks to the newspapers), money presents amounting to far more than the sum of the disputed taxes; but this does not alter the character of the original proceeding. They are decidedly "original characters"; and they come from what may well be called, even for Connecticut, a decidedly original family. Their mother Hannah Haddassah Hickock, only child of of David Hickock, of South Britain, five or six miles from Newtown, in the latter part of the last century, was married to Zephaniah Hollister Smith, then a clergyman settled in Newtown. He was a native of Glastonbury, and a marked character. We have been told that, owing to a difference arising between him and his church members, he excommunicated the whole church,—and they in turn dismissed him. This account is apparently not confirmed by the surviving members of his family, who say he abandoned the pulpit from conscientious motives—he disliked to receive money for preaching the gospel. After giving up preaching he, with his wife, went to live on the farm where his wife had lived, at South Britain—but he abandoned that region, two years later, and went to Glastonbury, where he opened a "country store" in that part of the township called Eastbury. It would appear that he also began then, or soon after, to read the law, with Judge Brace (father of the late Thomas Kimberly Brace, mayor of Hartford) who lived in the old Kimberly house and family, in Glastonbury, —with which family the Judge had become connected by marriage. This house, the present residence of the Smith sisters, a roomy old mansion built in 1739, is still in a sound and good condition. It, and the odly-shaped farm on which it stands, was bought by Mrs. Z. H. Smith, (mother of the "sisters") with money obtained by the sale of the South Britain farm; and that became thenceforth the residence of the Smiths.

Its singular shape is due to the form in which the Glastonbury lands were laid out and sold to the first settlers by the old Indian Sachem Sowheag, who lived where Middletown now is. In Barber's "Historical Notes of Connecticut" the boundaries of these original farms are quoted from the old Indian deed—each one "butting on the Great River, and running [easterly] three miles into the wilderness," (see Wethersfield town records,) and all being cut up into narrow strips, 22½ rods wide, and three miles long!—a shape like a lane or a

hoe-handle. The Smith farm is 22½ rods wide and three miles long,—being one of the few Glastonbury farms that have preserved their ancient shape. Zephaniah Hollister Smith was one of the old fedralists, and was known as a decided and active one in Glastonbury. He was the town lawyer for many years after his removal into the old Kimberly place. His wife also (a Fairfield county Hickock) was a woman of original character. She is said to have been a good astronomer, who made an almanac of the stars, and could always tell the time of night by the stars. By her star-knowledge of time, she has set the clock when it has stopped. She was also a writer of verse—(and her daughters are talking of having a book of her poems published. We present below a sample of her muse.) She learned French and Latin when a child; and at the decidedly mature age of fifty she took up the study of Italian, that she might read the Italian poets in their own tongue. Her linguistic tendencies were inherited by some, at least, of her children. There is an anecdote of Miss Julia to the effect that she was traveling once in a stage, in which for fellow-travelers she found a certain chancellor, accompanied by one of his learned friends. As the story goes, they, wishing to converse on some private business, began to talk in French, and were surprised to hear from the unknown woman the remark, "Excuse me, but I understand French." They then resumed their conversation in Latin, but were soon again interrupted by the remark, "Excuse me, gentlemen, I know the Latin." A good deal astonished, this time, they looked at the unknown in silence, and then once more fell to conversing, but this time in Greek. "If you'll excuse me," said the unknown woman, "I also understand the Greek." Thoroughly amazed, the chancellor (so runs the story) turned to her with the exclamation, "Who the d—l are you?" It is proper to add, even at the expense of spoiling a good story, that Miss Julia does not admit the entire correctness of this anecdote. She says she was riding in a stage to Sackett's Harbor; that Judge Kent, of Jefferson county, a brother of Chancellor Kent, was also a passenger; and that he, out of regard for her knowledge of the French language (of which she had been a teacher in the Troy seminary), and having learned that her mother understood the Italian, presented to her, for her mother, some beautifully bound Italian volumes.

The names of the five Smith sisters are as original as everything else in this original family. They have been occasionally published in a few newspapers, but seldom or never correctly. We will give them here: Hancy Zephina; Cyrinthia Sacretia;

Iaurilla Aleroyla; Julia Evelina; Abby Iaddassah. The two latter are the last of the family, and they are the "Smith sisters" — the last-named being the one whose name has acquired so much notoriety in the newspaper phrase of "Abby Smith's cows." And now, Miss Julia is likely to become equally as famous, but in another direction. She has translated the entire Bible—literally; going through the Hebrew and the Greek. She began this work in 1847—having her ideas first turned in this direction by "Millerism" and its excitement, which doctrine in those days was in full force. Miss Smith wished to see, for her own satisfaction, if there was any authority for "Millerism" in the original Hebrew. She found, of course, that there was not; but having got into the work, she acquired a zest for it, and after finishing the Old Testament, took up the New, and translated that literally from the original Greek; and then she went back and retranslated the Old, not only a second time, but a third, a fourth, and even a fifth time,—a task which it may be safely said, no one of this or any other age, man or woman, ever before accomplished, or ever dreamed of undertaking; and it will probable never be attempted by anybody else. So engaged did she become in her work that the dinnerbell would pass unheeded. The five translations were completed in seven or eight years. The work was never undertaken with any intention of publishing it, and it was not till last July that she first thought of this. The work is now going through the press of the American Publishing Company, Hartford, and is to be brought out next April. This work seems to make a new departure in several directions. It is not only the first translation of the Bible by a woman, but it is (or will be) the first work "set up" by a type-setting machine; and this machine is itself run by a woman —and another woman does the proof reading. Everything connected with this Bible seems to be on a new and original plan.

OUR GARDEN.

BY HANNAH H. SMITH.

[The following verses, referred to in the above article, were written many years ago, by the mother of Julia and Abby Smith of Glastonbury, in order to induce her husband to build a new fence around their garden. She had called his attention to the need of one, but he had failed to heed the request, so she called in the aid of the muses.]

But first of all, the garden wall
'Tis requisite to mention,
As we conjecture, its architecture
Is quite a new invention.

Part is so high, 'twould brave the sky,
Had not old Boreas shattered,
And rueful battle with the cattle,
Unfortunately battered.

One piece is pales, another rails,
But boards compose the front, all:
Some in particular, rise perpendicular
And some lie horizontal.

Next the inside, which forms the pride
Of curious cultivators
Where roses grow, and tulips blow
'Mid onions and potatoes.

Beside the bower, there's many a flower
And herb, in friendship twining;
Tomato blooms, with rich perfumes,
On beds of pinks reclining.

There satin-leaf, the garden's chief,
Near Caroline stands sentry;
Aspiring mullien, in garb of woolen,
Struts like merino gentry.

With hollyhock, catnip and dock,
By hoe, or spade, half murdered;
Some in straight line, some serpentine,
Are alleys lined, and bordered.

On either side, the paths divide
When pumpkin-vines attack them;
Through fennel, dill, and creeping gill,
'Tis difficult to track them.

You must proceed through tangling weed
Salute your footsteps' greeting,
For cornstalks rough, and bean-poles tough,
Prevent you from retreating.

But who can paint each herb and plant,
Or animals that eat them—
Pigs, calves and lambs, and oft their dams,
For there's no hound can beat 'em.

There's salad, greens, and hills of beans
For stringing and for shelling;
Where hens are scratching, turkeys hatching,
And scattered chickens yelling.

A row of peas, a flock of geese,
A piece of flax and clover—
A patch of oats, a dozen shoats
That range the garden over.

From the Windham Co. Transcript, Dec. 30, 1875.

FROM THE MISSES SMITH.—The following letter from the Misses Smith of Glastonbury, whose Alderney cows were attached and sold at auction to pay taxes—was addressed to a well known citizen of Danielsonville. We think it of sufficient general interest to warrant its publication :—

Glastonbury, Nov. 8th, 1875.

Dear Friend.—I do not, by any means, consider it a "losing operation" on my side to keep up a correspondence with you. Though I have had much else on my mind since I last wrote, I did want to write upon the receipt of your excellent letter. You still hold to your fifty women, and I am glad you think they can do better than I think they can. It is true they must be educated to know as much as men, and it is also true that their advantages to acquire an education grow better and better every year. It was altogether an unheard-of thing in our academy, when I went to school, for a girl to study the languages, but somehow I always wanted to do something contrary to the common course, and, though laughed at, stood it out bravely, never letting it be known how much I was mortified. I have since had it more than doubly made up to me in my gratification of reading the Bible in the three original tongues. I cannot express how greatly I enjoy the work of translating, and now the real meaning of different texts would thrill through my mind, till I could hardly contain myself; and now to bring it up again by having it published is no small satisfaction. The times are very much altered in respect to female education, and it is acknowledged to be quite honorable for woman to get knowledge, even to the understanding of different languages. And I, myself, seem even to be getting fame for having written out the Bible from the original tongues, so that I may yet get to be something besides Abby Smith's sister.

It is just two years ago to-day since Abby delivered her address in town meeting, and as I knew what it was, I went with her, little thinking of the turmoil it would occasion through the whole course of two years. Of all things that we should at our time of life get into law-suits, of which our father used to give us a dreadful idea, always advising his clients to keep out of the law, unless they were sure of a good cause.

You quote St. Paul more justly than many do, but we need not quote him at all in a wordly point of view, for literally we should not make him agree, but if we search out his spiritual meaning, there will probably be no confliction. "The letter killeth, but the Spirit giveth life" We think the Word of God speaks for the life to come, and not for the things of this world, and it becomes us to search out its true meaning, from its parables and dark sayings, which "the wayfaring man though a fool need not err therein."

You speak very encouragingly about their being tens of thousands of men enlisted on our side, if we have the prophetic vision to count them. Though we cannot see them we are not "disheartened or discouraged through our abuses and oppressions," for we have always believed that the truth will prevail, and we think it will show itself sooner than you have estimated, that is, "two decades of years."

We received a letter two or three weeks ago from a real worker for the Woman cause at Philadelphia, who wishes to engage a hundred copies of the coming Bible as soon as it is put forth from the press. She says with regard to the outlay of the money spent in printing the work, "I am connected with a great many benevolent enterprises, they all need money but for the advancement of the cause of women, in every direction, I know of nothing that would help us more than the translation of the Bible by a woman. This lady is editor of two monthly papers, one styled the Christian Woman, the other the Christian Child, and is president of the Woman's National Temperance Union,

JULIA E. SMITH AND SISTER.

From the Baltimorean, January 29, 1876.

THE "SMITH SISTERS."

We give in another column a communication from our learned and gifted townslady, Mrs. ALMIRA LINCOLN PHELPS. It is explanatory of an article upon the fourth page of to-day's BALTIMOREAN taken from the columns of the Hartford *Daily Times*, and possesses considerable interest for the general reader. The Misses SMITH have been quite prominently before the public during the past three years or more, because of their refusal to pay State and corporation taxes. They assigned as a reason, it will be remembered, their exclusion from the ballot-box, and their deprivation of those rights and immunities enjoyed by taxpayers. It will be seen that they are neither "disorganizers," nor "strong-minded" in the common acceptation of these terms, but most worthy, amiable and intelligent ladies.

THE SMITH FAMILY OF CONNECTICUT.

Editors of the BALTIMOREAN: In the "Hartford *Daily Times* " which I send you, is a truthful description of the " Smith family," two members of which have of late obtained notoriety for their independence in refusing to pay town taxes, which they considered unjust.

Though I do not advise women to resist the laws, nor seek to thrust themselves into the place of law makers, I do admit that the sisters, Julia and Abby Smith, had cause to complain of injustice. Their case is one of the exceptional ones, which, under the best system of laws, may exist. But the public should know who are those "low women," those *disorganizers of society*, whose names have been so widely vociferated in the newspapers of the day.

Among early recollections, few are more vivid and interesting than those of my intercourse with that family when the venerated and gifted parents, with their five daughters, each one a genius in her own specialty, were dwelling together in their hospitable and refined home, the whole forming a constellation of superior stars in an atmosphere of purity and intelligence.

ALMIRA LINCOLN PHELPS.

Eutaw Place, Jan. 21st, 1876.

From the Winsted Press, Feb. 3, 1876.

Those of our readers who are interested in the cause for which Abby and Julia Smith, of Glastonbury, are fighting, should not fail of reading their letter in another column.

A LETTER FROM GLASTONBURY.

Editor Winsted Press :—We thought by this time our friends in Litchfield county would like through your columns to hear from us again. We intended to have written last fall, supposing we should have something interesting to communicate, as there has been three cases brought before the Hartford courts against our selectmen for going contrary to their own laws in their eagerness to get our property, but it is impossible to bring them to trial. We never knew till last winter, that courts could be tampered with. Our lawyer said it made his hair rise to see the laws so trampled upon.

The past week for the first time, our rulers have given us a call. The first selectman, the collector, and another that we suppose they brought for a witness, for he said nothing. He was the one that measured off our meadow and charged $6.50 for running a straight line 30 rods, taking 20 minutes, with two assistants, for whose services he charged $1.50 apiece. He was asked what need of them and replied that the law allowed it. He is one of the justices.

The first thing, the collector demanded the tax, with much authority. We told him that as all our property was in the hands of the men, they could take what they pleased. We should not aid them in so doing, for nothing could be more unjust. He said we could not complain as it was so with all the women. We replied that did not make it right. That no women in this country or any other, that we had ever heard of, had ever been treated by their own townsmen as we had been ; such citizens too. After paying them so much money and assisting them every way we could, at our age, we must have seven of our cows seized and sold off at the sign post, which was the hardest trial, as every one was raised by my sister. And this was done after the collector had told us we might wait as long as we pleased before we paid, by paying one per cent a month, as we said we wanted to deliver our speech in town meeting first.

This the collector stoutly denied, which did not surprise us, having heard his testimony in court. We said they had waited several years on two men that owned factories and had lost several thousand dollars by it, which we had to help pay as well as the men. In our case there was no risk, but it would not do to let women go two months. "But," said he, "you had refused to pay." "Not then," we said, "we only wanted to wait till we could speak; but did that make any difference, when you had the whole in your hands? You knew you could take what you pleased when you sold at auction $2,000 worth of our meadow land for a tax of less than $50 to our greatest enemy, knowing him to be such at the time, for we had told you how he had carried off our winter apples." "He is one of the best men in town," replied the collector. The selectman urged very hard that we would pay the tax and end the business—we would "feel better," he said.

This tax is over $130. The one of last year of $150 is yet in court. It was assessed so contrary to law that nothing could be done about it. We answered Mr. Selectman "Would we feel better for doing wrong? Would our revolutionary forefathers have felt better to have paid the tax to Gt. Britain? They would have saved a seven years war, and thousands of lives. It was the same principle." "The British never meddled with the women—it was all the people," said he. "Are we not the people?" we answered again. "All we plead for is to stand on an equality with you before the law; to have the same privileges and immunities." "You do by your representatives." said he. "We have no representatives; we never voted for any; we have no interest in town affairs, having no voice in them," was our reply. "But you can see whether they have done correctly with respect to your property by examining the books," he continued. "But," said we "of what use would that be, as long as we cannot alter them? We have but one right given us by town or state, for all the money we have paid. We can petition the legislature, and we did, and they gave us *leave to withdraw!* We had not a man in the place to stand up for us." This was denied. But the town showed they endorsed the whole business, by putting in the collector again representative after he had seized our cows. It was some consolation to us to be supported by unknown friends in all parts of the country, for our story had reached the farthest border.

"But the whole country," we told them "is this year going to rejoice and honor our forefathers for standing out and setting up in this land the grand principle that 'Taxation without representation is tyranny,' and 'Governments derive their just powers from the consent of the governed,' Has not the spirit of those famous men descended to their daughters as well as their sons, have they not as keen a sense of right, and do they not feel as unwilling to be governed wrongfully? Have they ever received the least benefit from their forefather's labors? Better for them to have remained under England!"

My sister told them she would never have published her Bible had not the town used us so ill. They must have gone upon the ground that woman has not as much intellect as man and cannot take care of her property; but this work would show that a woman could do what no man had ever done, alone, and what is considered by all the greatest of works. They left without any hard words from Mr. S., and we can hardly believe, this centennial year, that he will give another warrant to the collector, to distress us as he has done.

Perhaps your readers may not know that we have contracted with the American Publishing Company, Hartford, to publish my sister's Bible, translated many years ago, when there were five sisters of us, and one friend now living in Wethersfield. We met together weekly to search the Scriptures, and were earnest to know the literal meaning of every word from the original languages, in which God had spoken to us. Seeing by the margin that the 47 translators of King James' Bible had not done so. My sister Julia first translated the Greek New Testament, then the Septuagint, (an older copy of the Bible than can now be found in the Hebrew language,) word for word, without giving any sense of her own, but let the dead languages speak for themselves. Knowing that they could not now be altered, and their construction is so perfect that one who understands them cannot get out of the way.

These three tongues—Latin, Greek and Hebrew—were written over the head of our Savior, and my sister rendered them into English five times, solely for the gratification of herself, the other three sisters and our friend. We all agreed that she made the text much clearer, putting the same English word for the same Hebrew or

Greek word. She was so much gratified to find that the whole Scriptures agreed from Genesis to Revelations, and was so well paid for doing it that she never thought it could be printed, until the town so lawlessly sold off our land last summer. We then thought we would let them see that one woman had done more than any man had ever done, alone, if they would not allow us to manage our own property.

Our Hartford bank stock will pay the $4,000 for the printing of one thousand copies and relieve us of one half our taxes, if we do sell them for $2.50 a copy. Of course we shall not get pay for printing unless we have another edition. It looks now by the letters we receive from all parts of the country, as if another edition would be called for. This one cannot come out till April, a Bible is so large a work.

ABBY H. SMITH AND SISTER.
Glastonbury, Ct., Jan. 24, '76.

From the Woman's Journal, Feb. 5, 1876.

ANOTHER RAID ON THE SISTERS SMITH.

EDITORS JOURNAL.—Having seen, in the Hartford papers, an incorrect account of a call made on us, last Wednesday, by the first selectman of this town, the collector, and, for a witness, the man who charged $9.50 with two assistants, for measuring a straight line of thirty rods, taking twenty minutes time; saying, when asked why he had two assistants,' "that the law allowed it to him," and this money he received in costs taken from us. We concluded it best, that, if you thought so too, the truth should be told in your JOURNAL. They came in after ten o'clock, A. M., and the collector commenced sternly, "I demand your tax." Abby was called, and gave her reasons, how contrary to right it was to pay it; and Julia said, they could take what they pleased; she ought not to take the trouble to go to Hartford and get the money, for that would be consenting to injustice. The selectmen said it would be better for us to pay our taxes; we should feel better. What! to do wrong? said Abby. Would our revolutionary ancestors have felt better to have yielded to taxation? which they declared to be tyranny, and endured a seven years war, and yielded up their lives for it. Did not women as well as men inherit this spirit? And this Centennial year they were going to rejoice over this principle! And did Great Britain use our forefathers anything like so badly as our town had used us?

The selectman gave answer; "It was the people they so used?"

We replied,—were not we the people? and we had no representation?

He said we had; our town represented us.

Did they represent us? Were they not all against us? Did they not vote in this very collector for town representative, who had so ruthlessly seized our pet cows, who spoke against us in the assembly to which we had been advised to apply to for relief?

He declared that he had never spoken a word, and the selectman seemed not to know that he had voted against us. We said "Mr. Miller the other representative did not." We told the story over, how shamefully we had been used by the collector, in seizing our cows and selling our land to our worst enemy, for a trifle, after he had told us we could let the tax lie by paying one per cent a month; which last he flatly denied, and said the one who took our land was one of the best men in town.

We gave the first selectman credit for being mild and polite; he made no threatening, neither did he offer an argument contrary to what we said, or allow that the town was against us. We parted in a friendly manner, and one would think by his agreeable demeanor that the town would not proceed to extremities against us, this Centennial year; but, by the articles of the nameless correspondents in the Hartford papers, the struggle is threatened to be renewed. They should have said, continued, for it has not ceased; our three cases in court are still there, and have been since last June. An unknown correspondent in the *Courant* asserts, that we had refused to pay another tax in this town, and said so to the town authority. When they asked us if we did, we told them positively that we did not refuse; that there was no need; they owned all our property, and in the name of taxes could take what they pleased.

The Collector told us, when he was here the last time before this, that he could take all we had if he chose. It was also stated in that paper that we told the town officers that some gentleman here offered money enough to contest the matter to the bitter end, and we were determined to do it. The whole of it was an out-spoken fabrication. I wrote a note yesterday to correct the statement, and doubtless the editors will have the fairness to do it. I was told yesterday by a subscriber to the Daily *Courant*, to demand the name of such a correspondent. I replied, that I did not care to know the name, for it might be one I never answered, and I should be satisfied to see my correction in print.

JULIA E. SMITH AND SISTER.
Glastonbury, Ct.

NOTICE—Taken by virtue of an Execution to me directed, and will be sold at Public Vendue to the highest bidder, at the public sign post in the town of Hartford, Conn., near the State House, twenty-one days after date, which will be on MONDAY, the 17th day of April, A. D. 1876, at 11 o'clock in the forenoon, to satisfy said execution and my fees thereon, the following described property, to wit:—one share of stock in the Phœnix National Bank of Hartford, Conn.

RUSSELL S. COWLES, Deputy Sheriff.
Dated at Hartford, this 27th day of March, 1876.

From the Hartford Daily Times.
To the Editor of the Times.

A notice is given in your paper, that by virtue of an execution on one share of stock in the Phœnix National bank, of Hartford, would be sold to the highest bidder at the public sign post in Hartford, without mentioning to whom that stock belonged. I merely wish to let your readers know that it was the property of Julia and Abby Smith, of Glastonbury.   COM.

From the Hartford Daily Courant.

A share of Phœnix National bank stock belonging to Misses Julia and Abby Smith of Glastonbury will be sold at public auction April 17th, at the public sign post in this city, by virtue of an execution. Has the collector found it easier realizing from bank stock than cows?

From the Woman's Journal, April 3, 1876.
NO LAWS FOR CONNECTICUT WOMEN.

EDITORS JOURNAL.—A year ago or more you gave an account of the illegal attachment and sale of eleven acres of our meadow land, for a tax of less than fifty dollars. Two able lawyers of Hartford read us the law, which expressly says that personal property must be first taken, and that we had the right to take advantage of the laws. We did so, and an able and upright justice of this town decided the case according to law. To the surprise of every one who heard the trial, the cause was appealed to the Court of Common Pleas, at Hartford, and was tried by George G. Sumner, though he was not the regular judge, who, we were told was sick. This was utterly false, for he was trying a case in another part of the building. This Mr. Sumner heard the case for three days in the severity of winter, or pretended to do so, for some of the witnesses said that when the testimony on our side was before him, he generally turned to look out of the window; and we ourselves also observed it. The fact was clearly proved that there was movable property enough to satisfy the tax and a great deal more, but the judge decided against us, after waiting two weeks, so as to prevent the case from going to the Court of Errors. He gave no reasons whatever for such injustice, but told our lawyer that he would look up the facts, and he should have them soon. Mr. Cornwall followed him up from day to day with the most extraordinary perseverance and patience, but at last Sumner said that the papers were all lost or stolen, and the case could not come up before the Court of Errors.

Judge Sumner was employed in the lobby business in the case of our town *versus* Wethersfield, at the New Haven Assembly, which cost Glastonbury $2000., and there is no question in our mind that he was put on the bench as a contrived plan, as he would not dare to give the case against the town in favor of two defenceless women who had no vote.

Last Friday Russell S. Cowles, the Deputy Sheriff, living in the south-east quarter of the town, six miles from the centre, who doubtless was put in to do this disagreeable business, called with an execution of $50 dollars twenty-seven cents, the cost of these unlawful doings. He is a man of more intellect than George C. Andrews, the Collector who seized our cows, and seems to discern right from wrong, and, we believe, in sincerity he advised us to pay this bill, and thereby, as he said, save ourselves trouble and much cost. We told him that the men had broken their own laws to get our property, and we considered it the worst kind of robbery, for the robber could come but once and then the whole community would be after him, but here there would be no end to it, if we quietly paid, and we should go contrary to our own conscience in aiding and abetting wrong doing. We also related to him the plea against the weak and defenceless, of such a man as Judge Waldo, who pleaded that these two women could own no personal property, for we were assessed as the heirs of Hannah H. Smith, who had died too long ago for us to inherit movable estate from her. And, yet, when the cows were seized, it was in the name of Hannah H. Smith's heirs, and they were raised several years after her death. The town assessors gave us that name to avoid the repetition of so many names; though there are but two of us left, we are still assessed by that designation. In the first place Judge Waldo said he could prove that we did not own our land at all, but after making a good deal of fuss in asking questions about it, we knew not to what purpose, he had to give it up.

But we do not think his argument had any effect upon the judge,.though we were told that Mr. Sumner was óne of his students in his law-office, for the whole proceedings of the court looked like underhanded contrivance, and we believe the case was decided before the trial.

The Deputy Sheriff called first, more than a week ago, and we have consulted with our lawyer, who was much surprised that the execution should be sent to us without his knowledge. He says he should have satisfied it without making us trouble, and advises us to pay it, for the law obliges us to do so and we cannot avoid it. He gives us such advise, no doubt out of feeling for us, for he thinks they will do all they can to annoy us, by attaching such things as will try us greatly and will make us much more expense. If our health and life are spared we think we can bear it, though it is an unlooked-for trial to us, that we are obliged to fight our native town, which we. always thought to be friendly to us, and whose prosperity we had cared for so much.

The cost of their last injustice and illegal doings, in the matter of a less than fifty-dollar tax, is over a hundred nineteen dollars, beside the tax. If they make a raid on our land or goods, there is no telling how much more this rascally business will amount to. There is already a $300 tax hanging over our heads, for which Collector Andrews claimed he could take all the property we owned. If we live long enough we may be ousted from our pleasant home, though if any one could see the unknown correspondence — letters upon the bible concern, they would think we might receive enough to furnish a supply for all necessary wants. We had one last night upon the same subject, from a woman living in Paris, Texas. She seems to think us much better off for not being married; for she says. she has supported her husband for eleven years, and has been teaching meanwhile, so that she has acquired a handsome property. Now he claims half her earnings for his children, who all have homes, the youngest forty years old, and the law of Texas allow it. In answering her letter, we told her that the laws here would allow her husband to take the whole, and put the young children where the mother could never see them again, which we hope will comfort her for not living in New England.

When the execution is levied you may hear from us again, as women have no redress but to publish their wrongs and let them travel over the nation.

JULIA AND ABBY SMITH.
Glastonbury, Ct.

From the Hartford Daily Courant.

A NOTICE IS ON THE SIGN POST IN the 4th school district in Glastonbury, that five Alderney cows are to be sold at public vendue to the highest bidder, by George C. Andrews, collector, Saturday the 15th of April , at 2 o'clock, p. m. They are the property of Julia and Abby Smith, and they invite their Hartford friends to take some refreshments with them at their home, as they still hold the old mansion house. The sign post is a half mile below their residence.

Glastonbury, April 10, 1876.

There was an auction sale of $165 of one share of Phœnix bank stock, in front of the state house yesterday, to satisfy a tax assessment on the Smith sisters of Glastonbury, who refuse to pay taxes because they do not believe in "taxation without representation." But the laws of the state must be enforced.

From the Hartford Daily Courant, April 28, 1876.

While celebrating the small beginings of a hundred years since, it will never do to underrate the small beginnings of to-day. Otherwise we may cast a slur on the next jubilee. Our women furnish music for the Centennial as they did their share of substance for the revolution, and they are likely to furnish music for routine politicians in the near future. The annual seizure and sale of the cattle of unrepresented tax-payers in Glastonbury worthily attracts the attention of THE COURANT's correspondent. Quite a bevy of women were present, one, certainly from Hartford, and the occurrence is talked of in families in the old liberty party way. These women, so far as I can see, seem to be of the same pattern with our sturdy grandmothers of the revolution. We may laugh at that auction, if we please, and the way the cows of the persistent Misses Smith after they were bidden in "put for home with nothing but tails and dust to be seen." But let us consider the grist of this woman's rights question for a minute. What father of these times will wish to die leaving property to daughters who are incompetent for civil action; leaving them nothing but their nails to depend upon to defend themselves unless they hire a man? All culture and education revolts at that. Women as well as men must be trained to use the power of civility. Seeing we have gone so far with popular suffrage, the only hope and legitimate end for it as well as popular law is to let the women have a vote. Probably not one half the sex want to vote, or know enough to want to, and that's a great argument in favor of their being put to that school. But the women should understand that the greater opposition to their voting comes from a very natural desire on the part of the best men to give our politics a good scourging first.

———

From the N. Y. Tribune, April 24, 1876.

THE MISSES SMITH'S COWS.

The cows of the Misses Smith of Glastonbury, Conn., have been sold again. They are Alderneys, small but serviceable. Last week the ruthless tax-collector came and levied on the three "milky mothers." Two of them the Misses Smith bid in; a third seems to have been carried off by some outsider. So there was not absolute and complete desolation in the barnyard of the Misses Smith. In addition to this, certain bank stocks of these firm ladies have lately been so d for taxes. The Misses Smith are determined they will pay no taxes until they are permitted to vote. Cows and bank stock are as nothing in comparison with this inestimable privilege of the ballot.

We are perfectly free to say that we admire the pluck of the Misses Smith. It is true that obstinate women are by no means rare in this wilderness of a world; but real martyrs, true to their convictions, even to the loss of cows and bank stock, are not so common. Unfortunately, it is also true that these heroines are to some extent the victims of a fallacy. The male variety of the human species pays taxes without representation on its property always until it is out of its nonage, and not unfrequently afterward. The Misses Smith forget that in a case like theirs, it is the property which pays the tax and not the owner of it. If a New-York man owns land in Massachusetts he must settle with the tax-collector of Massachusetts, albeit he has no representation in the General Court of that State. Whether the ladies of Connecticut vote or not, the State must look after their cows, protecting them from all Rob Roys and other raiders, also protecting the edifice in which they are housed from the midnight incendiary. When the State taxes the cows, it is for taking care of them. Constables are appointed. Justices of the Peace are commissioned, and jails are built for the sake of defending the right and title of the Misses Smith to their pretty Alderneys. They are asked to pay a moderate sum for this service, and they peremptorily refuse. "Very well then," says the State, "I will take the cows." A legal vendue follows, and the Misses Smith buy in the animals. In this way they do really pay the taxes,

but they have the sweet satisfaction of having their own way, a pleasure which is said to be promotive of longevity. So we suppose that the Misses Smith cows will continue to be sold for many years to come.

The theory of taxation is that property, whether of male or female ownership, must pay. Frequently taxes are assessed upon land or chattels the precise ownership of which is unknown. What the collector wants is the money. He doesn't care a penny who pays it. Suppose the Misses Smith should take it into their heads to commit a theft. Would it be a sufficient answer to the indictment that they were not represented in the Legislature which passed the law against larceny?

———

From the New Haven Journal and Courier, April 24, 1876.

LETTER FROM JULIA AND ABBY SMITH.

To the Editor of the Journal and Courier:

We have many acquaintances in New Haven County, and we want to tell them how their old friends have fared in their latter years in Glastonbury, where they were born and brought up, and supposed that none had more cordial friends in their native place. As State and town are against us, we can expect no aid only in sympathy and advice. We still do not believe that a majority of the voters here know how infamously the ancient citizens of this town are used, for everything is kept as private as possible with respect to us. Not a man of this place has ever dared to speak our names in a public meeting, since we have been so outrageously attacked as to cows and meadow land. Some four or five weeks ago, to our surprise, a deputy sheriff of this town, living six miles from the centre, probably put in for this express purpose, called on us to pay an execution, in consequence of the men breaking their own laws, and by underhanded management changing the regular judge of the court of common pleas, and getting George G. Sumner to take his place, who had been lobbying for the town in the legislature against Wethersfield, and had cost Glastonbury $2,000. The man of course could not hear to the law for two defenceless women against a whole town who had just paid him so much money, and decided the case contrary to law and testimony, and gave not a reason for such an unjust and illegal decision, and promised to give the facts of the case to Mr. Cornwall, our lawyer, so that he could bring it up to the court of errors. After following him up from day to day through the spring and summer, Mr. Cornwall was foiled, for Sumner would do nothing at all, declaring the papers were all lost. And after all, an execution was made out by our persecutors, without the knowledge of our lawyer, who said had they sent it to him he should have paid it, for the law could enforce it. We told the deputy sheriff we could not conscientiously advance the money for such nefarious doings, and he grew pious at last and said we must forgive our enemies, and do good to them that hated us, &c., &c. We replied we must resist the devil, or he would certainly come again, and this was all the devil's work. He assented to it, but wanted to save us expense and trouble, and said we could as well write about it in the papers, if we did pay it. He left us the last time three weeks ago yesterday, went to Hartford advertising in one of the newspapers that he had levied an execution on a share of Phœnix bank stock for $100, the amount and costs, to be sold at public vendue at the sign post in Hartford, the 17th of April. He took care none should know for what reason he had attached the share or to whom the property belonged, dating at Hartford, not even mentioning our names, so that we had to get a notice printed in the same paper that our friends might know that we owned the property. Yesterday we went to Hartford through the floods and attended the auction, against the advise of our lawyer, who said women did no go to auctions, but we do not let our property be sacrificed in this way without seeing to it, neither do we let it pass without talking of the robbery. We stood by the young man who beat the drum and heard him say he did not want such business and wanted to get through as soon as possible. In the meantime we have had a greater trial than this. A week ago last Saturday night that same old collector came and drove away our Alderney cows again for a tax of $131.73. He seized five which we told him might double in number in a week. He demurred at our wanting two left, but he grew a little more lenient and left the two we begged for, as one had a young calf. They were kept near the sign post a half mile below here. I went to see them three mornings and found a fine calf among them the second day. The man who kept them has not lived in town a great while and made many excuses for taking them, said the collector did not tell him until he agreed to keep them whose stock they were, and then he asked him about it. He said they should have the best of care and I think he kept his word. We understood that George C. Andrews, the collector, took up the whole day in trying to get somebody to take them; not one of our old neighbors would do any such thing. We attended the cow auction last Saturday, without being summoned by

dog and drum, as at the New Year's day seizure two years ago. Several ladies were there for our solace, and four men spoke to us, two of whom were strongly on our side. The bidding off of the three best cows sufficed to pay the tax and costs, which together were $163.40. We bought back two of the cows as mementoes of the first auction block sale, though they may be taken and sold again, as another tax has been sent to us by mail of $96. The pretty little calf was not sold, but I dare not raise it to be liable to such outrages to the feelings in future. We returned home to get some quiet till Monday, telling our friends who stopped to see us that here was a fine commentary on the resistance of our forefathers to taxation without representation a hundred years ago, and now a whole country were up in arms for rejoicing to celebrate the fortitude and bravery of our ancestors, while for asserting the same principles two lone women are forced to be present in little over two years at four public auctions, two of them to sell cows raised by one of them, and one to bargain off $2,000 worth of meadow land for a tax of less than fifty dollars, and the other to sell off bank stock by execution by men disregarding their own laws. JULIA AND ABBY SMITH.

GLASTONBURY, April 18, 1876.

From the Woman's Journal, April 29, 1876.

THE SISTERS SMITH—COW AUCTION NO 2.

EDITORS WOMAN'S JOURNAL.—We promised to give a sequel to the deputy sheriff's proceedings. But really we cannot begin where we left off, for there has been a succession of infamous doings, and they must be related as they come into mind. We have just returned from Hartford, where we have been to attend the auction to sell bank stock, and last Saturday, that is Sunday between, we were called to another auction sale of our Alderneys again. They took five, but sold only three, which satisfied the tax and costs amounting to $163.42, the tax, $131.73. We had to buy back two cows, and let one go. We did not wish to part with all that were seized the first time, though they may be driven from us again, for they have sent in another tax, by mail, of $96, which it is said must be paid this month.

The same old collector came on Saturday, the week before, to demand the tax. We told him he must do as he pleased, as he claimed that he could take all we had; he said it was lawful. We both followed him to the yard and told him the cows ought not to be taken at this time, for by keeping them a week there might be double their number. He was more lenient this time, for at our special pleading he left us two, and drove the rest near the sign post, where he got a man to keep them. The second time I went to see them, there was a fine little calf there lying by its mother.

We were much surprised that a man living within half a mile of us would take them; his wife said she was afraid we should not like it, and he said he agreed to do it before he knew whose they were, for the collector did not tell him, until he asked him. He promised to take the best care of them, and we believe he did so. We do not think the collector could have got another place, for we understood he was out all the day along street, and it was nearly night before he drove them away.

The auction was held at 2 o'clock P. M., but there was neither dog nor drum, this time, but quite a concourse at the sign post, who looked as if they came to make disturbance, but were somewhat afraid to do so, and said nothing worth minding. There were several ladies, whose conversation helped us much, and four men spoke to us, and two showed they were on our side. We told them the scene was quite a comment upon this Centennial year, when the whole nation was to rejoice for the resistance of our forefathers to taxation without representation, a hundred years ago.

There is another collector appointed, to take hold of our property for the coming tax, so that it will not be so disagreeable to see a new one, and he cannot go more contrary to the laws than this one has done. The affair has been a fine display of town authority, and we must call it the whole town, for not a man has dared speak in our favor in any public meeting, or even to mention our names. We do not think half the voters have the least idea of the unfeeling usage we have received. These auctions are kept as private as possible, and nobody would know of such unjust and lawless treatment did we not tell of it ourselves.

As to the sequel of the deputy sheriff's business, he called for the last time, three weeks ago to-day. He stopped in the morning to plead with us to pay the execution, which he could not prevail on us to do, and at last grew pious, quoting texts of scripture, that we must love our enemies and do good to them that hate us, &c. We told him we must resist the devil or he would not flee from us, and would come again, and this was all the devil's work, to which he assented, but said it would save us much trouble and expense, and then he said we could write an account of it just as well if we paid it. He left us very politely, and called again at night, and said he had levied on a share in Phœnix bank, the bill was $80.27 instead of $50, as was by some mis-

take printed in the JOURNAL, and he had advertised it in one of the Hartford papers.

Two days afterwards, we found that it was put in without saying to whom the stock belonged, or what the levy was for, or even mentioning the town of Glastonbury at all. We put in the same paper that the shares belonged to Julia and Abby Smith of Glastonbury, for the information of our friends. Though we are in the hands of those who keep everything as secret as possible, we let it all out, to their great annoyance, for they are somewhat sensible of the disgrace. The whole cost in this case of the men s breaking their own laws to get our property is over $139, beside the tax which was not quite $50 in the first place, and the cost of the two cow auctions $71, making $210 beside the regular taxes.

All the proceedings of the town against us have been contrary to laws men have enacted for their own benefit, (unless it is this last tax,) and they cannot be severe enough against the weak and defenceless, without breaking these very laws. There has just come to our knowledge a poll-tax sent to a poor widow, whose husband died the last of Nov. 1875, and a few days ago another poll-tax has been sent with a tax upon the estate of the husband, who served three years in the war of the rebellion. They must have known it was all contrary to law, but they did not think this bereaved widow would know it. Her husband estate was prized at 600 dollars, all in real estate, and she is entitled to the use of a third, with a baby of seven months' old, and no work to be obtained. Any one would say that in such a case a tax should be abated, if the selectmen have any idea of what is right.

In a little over two years we, who have paid more money into the town treasury than anybody else, have been forced to attend four auctions, to see our propety worse than stolen from us, when we have never broken a law on the statute book, that we know.

JULIA AND ABBY SMITH.
Glastonbury, Conn.

From the Winsted Press, May 4, 1876.

THE GLASTONBURY LADIES AGAIN.

Editor Winsted Press:—We want our Litchfield County friends to hear from us again and will give you a few more last words, though we think they may not be the last as matters go on now, for we seem to be right in the midst of the battle, and there may be as many more last words as were ascribed to Mr Baxter. We write under some excitement just now, as we have just had five of our Alderney cows driven out of our yard again to be sold at the sign post to the highest bidder, a half mile below here, next Saturday at 2 o'clock, p. m. We have one of us been down to see them the second time this morning and found a fine calf lying beside its mother, and probably before Saturday there may be double the original number as we told the same old collector when he took them. He was somewhat more lenient this time as at our urgent request he did leave two, though he said that one was enough for we were but one family, but as there was a calf belonging to one it would have been some trouble to take calf and all. We are now in the midst of two auctions. On account of that unjust and unlawful decision of Judge Geo. G. Sumner, put on the bench on purpose to try this case, the cost was thrown upon us, though he promised our lawyer that he would give him the facts of the case, so that he could bring it before the court of errors, but he never would, saying the papers were lost; neither did he ever give any reason for his illegal decision. The costs in this case amount to over 30 dollars, and there is to be another auction at the sign post in Hartford next Monday, the 17th, at 1 o'clock p. m., to sell a share of Savings Bank stock. The deputy sheriff of the town, who lives in the south-east quarter, six miles from the center, appointed, we suppose, on purpose to serve this execution, who has more intellect than Andrews, the collector, and has more perception to see injustice, called and told us that he had put an advertisement in a Hartford paper. He took care that the name of Glastonbury or our names should not appear in the notice of the vendue, and we had to write and tell our friends that the stock belonged to Julia and Abby Smith of Glastonbury, and it so came out in the next issue. They kept as whist as can be about their shameful usage of us and endeavor to keep things hid, but these women let it all out and this is the way they disgrace the town as they are accused of doing. We did not believe the selectman, who was so pleasant when he called last winter, would give another warrant to disturb us, when we have done nothing only what our forefathers did a hundred years ago, resist taxation without representation, and now how their memory is to be glorified for these doings. But it is awful, even in this centennial year, for two defenceless, law-abiding women to assert these principles.

JULIA AND ABBY SMITH.

Glastonbury, April 11, 1876.

From the Ballot Box Toledo, O., May 1876.

LETTER FROM THE MISSES SMITH.

MRS. S. R. L. WILLIAMS, EDITOR OF THE BALLOT BOX: — We congratulate you upon the issue of this new paper, which came to us last night, and we can not but endorse the spirit of its contents, and send enclosed one dollar for its continuance, addressed to Julia and Abby Smith, Glastonbury. Ct. It was somewhat a solace to our feelings, which had just before been stirred up by another raid of that notorious collector George C. Andrews upon five Aldeney cows, which at 6 o'clock he drove off out of our yard and put them into a Mr. Robinson's, a half mile below, to be sold at the same old auction block next Saturday, at 2 P. M., for a tax, he said, of $131.73.

We want to say a good deal to you, to put in your paper, but you cannot afford much space to such far off writers.

When the collector called last winter, with the first selectman, we told Mr. Samson that my translation of the Bible would never have been printed had we been used civilly by our town, for it was never written for the public; but they had forced us to do it, to show that we were capable of taking care of our own property, for one of us, without aid from anybody, had done what no man alone ever had, and they had obliged us to take all our bank stock in Hartford to pay for it, and if we never sold a volume, we should be rid of half our taxes. We expect the work will come out next week for distribution. We thought it would be done before; and we have so many letters about it that it is possible after all that we shall get remunerated, though this first thousand will bring us in debt $2,500.

Our cow auction we are to attent next Saturday, and the Monday after another auction at Hartford, seven miles from here, to sell bank stock to satisfy an execution of over $80, which is to cost $100 before they get through. This is most unlawful and outrageous business from beginning to end, owing to the collector's taking meadow land for a tax of less than $50, instead of personal property, which their own laws say expressly must be done. Then by changing the judge and putting one in of their own selection, he decided the case wholly contrary to law, to throw the cost upon two defenceless women. The deputy sheriff pleaded hard to have us pay the execution, but we told him we could not conscientiously do it. He grew pious, and said we must love our enemies and do good to them that hated us, &c. We told him we must resist the devil or he would not flee from us, and it was all the devil's work. He assented to that, but it would save us much expense and trouble. He put the advertisement in such a way, in a Hartford paper, not giving Glastonbury or our names in it at all, so that we had to send a notice to the same paper that the bank stock belonged to Julia and Abby Smith, of Glastonbury, and we wanted our friends to know it. We were determined that such doings should not be hidden. We shall attend it ourselves, and think there will be some noise arise from it, the slyness of the sheriff notwithstanding.

JULIA AND ABBY SMITH.

Glastonbury, Ct. April 9, 1876.

Petition of Julia and Abby Smith presented in person to the Gen. Assembly of the State of Conn., and read by order of the speaker the 24th of May 1875.

ABBY SMITH AND SISTER.

The following memorial was read :
"Julia E. Smith and Abby H. Smith earnestly petition the General Assembly of this state, in whose power they are, that they would grant them the same privileges and immunities enjoyed by the other citizens of this state, their money having been taken. The same for all the state's improvements, which has never given them but one right in return—the right of petition. And upon this right they pray that their property may not be taken from them as it has been without their having any voice in it, or any appeal to a higher power (as state and town are equally interested in doing it), leaving them without a country to help them, or any state who acknowledges them as citizens, or would protect them as such. They entreat the assembly to grant them the same privileges that our forefathers entreated the Parliament of Great Britain to grant, a hundred years ago, and for which they suffered a seven years' war to obtain, and are now celebrating their victory with great display throughout the town. Your petitioners pray that they also may be permitted to join in the triumph of the great principles honored by the whole nation, that "taxation without representation is tyranny," and "governments derive their just powers from the consent of the governed."

Glastonbury, May 17, 1876.

From the Hartford Daily Times, May 23, 1876.

Julia Smith's Bible, just published, has called forth the following criticism. It was not intended for publication, being an extract from a private letter; but it is so well put, and brief, withal, that we trust this correspondent will excuse its appearance in print :

My opinion of it is that it has power to reach to a substratum of thought at a depth beyond where King James's can reach; and this because of the Hebrew idiom. I have read only a little of it, but what I have read remains in my mind in the form of divinest wisdom dissociated from language, like the wisdom of a little child who has no words to pick and choose. How intensely I love a book where the ideas overtop the language.

From the Woman's Journal, Nov. 4, 1876.

CENTENNIAL DOINGS IN GLASTONBURY.

EDITORS JOURNAL :—The town has taken our cows again. It seems most astonishing such an outrage can be committed in the middle of the day, this professed year of rejoicing; that these animals, well known to all, as belonging to the most law abiding, well-doing citizens of the place, as we have ever been called, could be driven through its main street three miles, without one word of disapproval or inquiry from any of its men. It was done in the face of all the laws of liberty and equality ever passed by the nation, and of all their glorification of these laws!

Their new collector Adelbert Crane called the last time, in July. We told him we had heard he would take our cows again. He said he had told no man living what he intended to do; he should do as he thought best, without anybody's advice; he should call again, however. We have watched every man coming near our house ever since—that is all summer, dreading the man with one arm. He has lost an arm working in the factory, but looks large, fat and lazy. He came round our house last night with another man. and they went out to the man milking. Of course we went out too, to learn what he was going to do; for, having a case in the Hartford Court, we told him we must know. He told us it was not necessary for us to be at home. This morning he was at the same place before breakfast. We told him, if he took our cows, he must leave us the one which had a little calf in the stable, and the other three would bring the tax, which was ninety six dollars and sixty five cents, for none would be sold under fifty dollars. We wanted him to leave this only, as the calf could not go so far.

The owners of the meadow on this river make common field of it after the 10th of October, depending upon it for their fall feed. But Crane told Mr. K. not to turn our cows in there, and learning from him that we had two yearling heifers there, he went with his boy after them. The field is half a mile wide and three or four miles long on the river, but he actually got them about noon.

In spite of all our entreaties, and we pleaded hard, he drove off the little calf with its mother,—wholly unnecessary: for he might have taken the other that he left, as well.

"Satan is the god of this world," the Bible says, and nothing looks more like it than to be robbed of our property in this way, sanctioned by law. We have never had the least desire to see the great things at Philadelphia, connected as they are with great principles professed, but entirely overlooked.

If our little calf lives through such ill treatment, we may tell you more about her in another letter.

JULIA AND ABBY SMITH.

Glastonbury, Ct.

From the Woman's Journal, Nov. 4, 1876.

THE CASE OF THE SISTERS SMITH.

It seems to me, that the repeated wrongs done to the Sisters Smith when their property has been sold for taxes, must be exposed, and if possible punished.

These sisters fully believe that they have been treated not only unjustly, but illegally.

For instance when their eleven beautiful acres of meadow land were sold for a tax of only fifty dollars, they went early to the auction with some friends, so that they might be ready to take advantage of any opportunity which might occur in their favor. But there was neither auctioneer, collector, nor any other person anywhere in sight.

Thinking it possible that these persons were at another place at a little distance, the sisters set forth for that place. But when in a few moments they looked back, they saw the auctioneer and others at the spot to which they went at first. They retraced their steps as fast as possible. The distance was only a few rods. But when they arrived they were coolly told that the land was sold. Neither they nor the friends who were with them had heard any call for a "bid" nor had they heard any "bid" made.

Such was the unseemly haste with which the auctioneer disposed of their fine tract of land for a paltry fifty dollars, and that too, to a man who had tormented them before to get possession of that very piece of land which he had long coveted.

This is only one instance of the unjust manner in which these aged women have been treated while they have stood for the defence of a great principle.

I have been too busy to communicate with them. But I am sure that a legal investigation should be made, without cost to them, while they are still able to be witnesses in their own behalf.

The election will shortly be over, and then there will be time for this case, which is that of a principle which involves all women. A few hundred dollars should be raised at once, to fee a lawyer who shall work up the case, and then the ablest

counsel that can be obtained should carry it through.

We will open a subscription in this office, and, from time to time, publish the names and the amounts contributed for this purpose. Small sums will be welcome. We can surely make up a fund to help settle by a legal trial, what it took seven years of war to establish, a century ago. Begin at once.

L. S.

From the Woman's Journal, Nov. 18, 1876.

NO ESCAPE FROM MERCILESS PERSECUTION WITHOUT SACRIFICE OF PRINCIPLE.

EDITORS JOURNAL:—After our article in your paper of the 4th inst. came out, we intended to have continued our narration of the doings of the unfeeling collector, Adelbert Crane, in the next number, but we did not get the JOURNAL until Wednesday, and Thursday at 9 A. M., we were called to attend the Court of Common Pleas, at Hartford, to try the validity of the action of the select men and assessors with respect to unlawful assessment of taxes and seizure of our real estate. The case had been set aside twice by our adversaries, much to our inconvenience. The 23d inst., at 2 o'clock P. M., the sale at the sign post was to take place, and we were on hand in due time. Though it rained, the collector waited for the first select man and two justices of the peace to make their appearance. He then set up the cow and calf, and had a man of his own to bid several times very low, and added a dollar more at a time. To put an end to this business I bid $120, and told the collector I supposed it was enough to cover the tax and cost, the tax being ninety-six dollars and sixty-five cents. He set up another cow at once, which was struck off to me for forty-one dollars, the amount for the two being $161. I had but $125 with me, and said, as he was coming up to our house, that I could pay it at home, but he immediately called out that the cows were not sold, and set them right up again, and he would take no bid of ours the second time, and we got Mr. Kellogg to bid, but he had no cash with him. At last he ordered me to go home and get it, giving twenty-five minutes time to go three quarters of a mile. By the fleetness of Mr. Kellogg's horse we did get back within one minute of the time, though I went to a neighbor's to get a little more, for I knew perfectly well if I failed by only fifty cents, all our stock would at once be sacrificed, for he held watch in hand, and a neighbor heard him say the time was about out. This was all done in the hearing of the select man and the two justices, and I paid the $161 in their sight, they not saying a word, when I have had many dealings with this head officer about the town poor, and he knew perfectly well that my word could be entirely depended upon. But here these men close by and a crowd of others and some ladies must all stay in the rain, for a defenceless woman (by no means helpless) to be sent off three fourths of a mile, when the insatiable collector had to come to our house with the stock he had not sold, and pay us an overplus of twenty six dollars and some cents, and until he had all things his own way I could not possibly find out an item of the cost, which was enormous; the needless driving of those two little yearlings out of the meadow, with keeping them a week, I think made twelve dollars expense.

When the collector got out of the house I asked if he was to collect the next tax, and Abby told him she should dread seeing him come in sight of the house. This man is a butcher and well knew the value of the stock and, no doubt, intended to have disposed of the whole for the tax and cost, before I could get back; though there was not a man there that could have paid down for them, for I could not borrow even two dollars from one of them. They said they were sorry, but that they had none.

But we had some advantage in my being sent home, for Abby walked about among the men, telling them here was an example of the noble principles of our forefathers being acted out, when the whole country were rejoicing on account of these principles, and that such usage was a disgrace to the town, which could never be effaced. None answered.

We got home from Hartford last night, where we have been to attend to our case before the Court of Common Pleas. It was finished Friday night, and we should think by the facts and pleas that it must be decided in our favor. We liked the appearance of Judge McManus, who gave his attention equally to both sides, which George G. Sumner did not. But this judge is of the same politics as our town; on that account he may be swayed to decide against us; but we have strong hopes that he will not. If he does, we must hold in our remembrance that we only yield up our property for sake of principle, when, for the same principle, our royal forefathers gave up their lives.

JULIA AND ABBY SMITH.
Glastonbury, Nov. 12, 1876.

From *the Woman's Journal, Nov.* 18, 1876.

KU-KLUX IN CONNECTICUT.

In another column will be found a very graphic account of the last encounter which the Sisters Smith have had with the tax collector of Glastonbury. It should be read by every one.

Nothing more dastardly can be found in all the records of Southern violence. It will be remembered that the Sisters Smith are old ladies, well educated, intelligently maintaining at any cost the rights which our revolutionary ancestors died to establish. Connecticut has had a large share in causing Centennial honors to be paid to these ancestors, but not a single official in that State, from the governor down, has ever yet given them the least help, but has left them to be plundered of their property in a shameful and brutal manner, and the principle they defend to be trampled under foot. Do the rulers and the political speech-makers of Connecticut cry out for an honest government, and a free vote at the South, so that the eyes of people may be turned away from the wrong they are themselves inflicting on two courageous women?

Nothing can be finer than the defence these sisters make. The final sentence of their account shows how well they know the ground on which they stand. It is this: "We must hold in remembrance that we only yield up our property, when, for the same principle, our royal forefathers gave up their lives."

This sentence deserves to be, and no doubt will be written under the historic picture which some future artist will make of this very scene, which the sisters to-day record in the WOMAN'S JOURNAL.

Abby Smith will soon have published in pamphlet form a narrative of all the transactions connected with the enforced sale of their property for taxes. It should be circulated everywhere, and be read by everybody, that all the people may see the need of Woman's right to the ballot.　L. S.

THE MISSES SMITH IN THE COURT OF COMMON PLEAS.

The case of the Misses Smith tried before a Glastonbury magistrate (Martin Hollister) in 1874, and decided in their favor, was carried before the Court of Common Pleas, Hartford, in February, 1875, on appeal by the defendant, George C. Andrews, a collector of Glastonbury. The indictment as carried before the Glastonbury magistrate by the Misses Smith was for "unlawful seizure of their land" by said collector. The first part of the trial (the appealed case in the Court of Common Pleas) was in regard to the location of the land that was seized; the details and manner of the sale; the names, and dates of decease, of the parents and sisters of Julia E. and Abby H. Smith. The father, who died in February

1836, was Zephaniah H. Smith; the mother, who died in December 1850, was Hannah H. Smith. The five daughters came in the following order: Hancy Zephina, who died in June 1871; Cyrinthia Sacretia, who died in August 1864; Laurilla Aleroyla, who died in March 1857; Julia Evelina and Abby Hadassah, the two surviving sisters. Judge Waldo, counsel for defendant, stated that his object was to show that these ladies (Julia and Abby Smith) were neither the owners nor possessors of this property. [In other words, that they did not own the farm on which they had lived all their lives, and which has never had any other claimants since their sisters died, and which would be theirs by right of possession—as Julia Smith aptly remarked—without any probating of wills, or without any will at all, as the law requires but 15 years possession to establish one's claim; and they had been in undisputed possession ever since their mother died a quarter of a century ago. However, perhaps the Judge may be excused in his strait to find a plea for the defendant, as he knew, as well as other lawyers who had looked at the case, that the law was wholly on the side of the Misses Smith, since it was plain to every one who knew them in Glastonbury, as well as to the collector, that there was plenty of movable property, which the law requires to be taken first. Reporter.]

The land seized by the collector included fifteen acres of their best meadow land, and was valued at about $2,000. This, the collector sold on the 20th of June 1874, for $78.35. Julia Smith testified that on the day of the sale, she and her sister drove down to the lot at the hour appointed, and after waiting an hour, the defendant, (Andrews) came on the lot with Mr. Talcott, surveyor, and Mr. Hardin, the man who bought the land, besides a couple of boys to help measure it off. That she went up to Andrews and told him it was unlawful to take the land as there was movable property, to which he replied that he had "already bargained for it," which greatly astonished her, as this was a further violation of law, the law requiring public bidding in sales of this kind, and not previous and private bargains in the matter. The following is from this part of her testimony, on the cross-examination:

I was utterly astonished, as I had supposed it was to be sold by public bidding at the time and place as advertised in the newspapers. My sister went up to the collector and said, "Why, Mr. Andrews, how can you do so wrong?" He replied, "I have engaged to do it." Then he said he should sell 80 rods west of the drain; "it is bargained for at $78.35—you can bid more if you choose." I said we could

not bid as it was an unlawful proceeding, and that he could not force us to break the law if he broke it himself. I told him we had consulted ex-mayor Robinson and lawyer Johnson, and they had said it was contrary to law to take real estate when there was movable property. After he had spoken about having made a bargain for it, he said, "Who bids?" Nobody bid. Then I asked who had got the land. He said Mr. Hardin had.

Mr. Cornwall, counsel for plaintiffs, introduced the original title-deeds, showing the transfer of the Anson Kimberly farm in Glastonbury in February 1796 to Hannah H. and Zephaniah H. Smith—Hannah H. buying two-thirds, and Zephaniah H., one-third. Then considerable testimony followed in regard to this property and the wills of different members of the family—the father and mother and the three sisters deceased. The property as originally bought included 133 acres of land, three miles long from east to west, and 22½ rods wide. The five sisters were the only heirs of their father and mother. In September 1846, ten years after their father's death, they gave their mother a quit-claim deed to the whole property. But it was all used in common as it always had been, and the mother at her death, left it to go to her heirs without a will. Since 1871, Julia E. and Abby H. have been the sole and undisputed possessors.

A long discussion, consuming some hours, was next carried on between counsel on both sides as to the rate-bill, or book of assessments of taxpayers of the town of Glastonbury, counsel for plaintiffs claiming that it did not meet the requirements of the law—that the rate-bill was not properly signed. All he could find was a signature to a copy of the votes of the town—which did not authenticate at all, the list of the Misses Smith. He claimed it would have been just as well for the select men to have signed the first chapter of Genesis. The court decided that the rate-bill conformed to the law.

Testimony of Mr. George C. Andrews, collector of Glastonbury. Direct examination by Mr. Goslee.

Q. You reside in Glastonbury?
A. Yes.
Q. What office did you hold during the years 1873 and '74, commencing with the 6th of October?
A. Collector.
Q. Will you state whether this book was placed in your hands as collector?
A. It was.
Q. Was there a tax against the heirs of Hannah H. Smith?
A. Yes; a tax of $49.83.
Q. What was the date of that warrant?

. 23d of February, 1874.

Q. Did you take any measures to notify the parties whose names are contained in tha book?

A. I advertised the tax in the Hartford Weekly Times, and the Weekly Courant, three times.

Q. Did you call upon the parties?

A. I called on the 18th of March, 1874, to collect the tax.

Q. Whom did you see?

A. Miss Julia and Abby Smith, and Mrs. Kellogg. Mr. A. M. Brainard went with me. When I asked them if they were ready to pay, Miss Abby said, "Of course we shall not pay it; we have received altogether too much encouragement." They went on to tell of the letters of encouragement they had received from all over the Union, and of the money they had also received, to encourage them to resist taxation. I asked them if they had any personal property to turn out which I might levy upon to satisfy the demands of the law. They said: "No; we shall have nothing to do with this infamous business."

Q. Who said this?

A. Miss Abby; though they were both talking most of the time.

Q. Did they say they had any personal property?

A No; they did not. Afterwards, on the 1th of April, I levied on their meadow land.

Q. Did you give them notice of that levy?

A. I called on them on my return from the meadow on the 11th of April.

Q. At this time, or prior to the levy, had you made any search for personal property?

A. I inquired of them in regard to personal property, but they didn't wish to give me any information. I had examined their farm tools, but all that I ever saw was in rather a poor condition.

Q. Did you find anything upon which you could levy?

A. No: nothing in my judgment sufficient to levy upon.

Q. You had been in the house?

A. Yes; and at the back of the house, towards the meadow.

Q. At what time of the year was this?

A. April.

Q. No great amount of hay and grain in the barn, was there?

A. No. I advertised in the Weekly Times, April 13, 1874.

Q. State what you did after that advertisement.

A. On the 20th of June I went down to their premises; hitched my horse in the street near Mr. Hardin's, and in company with surveyor, and assistants of Mr. Hardin's, went on the meadow lot. When once on the lot I was satisfied that I was on the land I had advertised, and opened the sale. It was 2 o'clock, or a little past. The ladies were there at once. They were west of us when we reached the lot, driving about in the grass, with horses and wagons.

Q. Did you, or any of your party go on the lot with teams?

A. None of us. I opened the sale by saying, "Gentlemen, I have levied upon this tract of land, and advertised for sale so much as is necessary to raise the tax and pay expenses. I stated to them that the tax and expenses were $78.35. I told them I proposed to sell the whole width of the land, commencing at the drain on the east, and going west as far as necessary to raise the money. I called on them to bid by rods. How many rods west of the drain would they take to pay the tax and expenses? Mr. Nelson A. Hardin said he would pay the tax and expenses for 80 rods west of the drain. At this stage of the proceedings, Miss Julia E. Smith came up to us and cautioned me not to sell it. I stated to Miss Smith's party, as they came up to us, that the land was up for sale, and that I had had a bid for 80 rods west of the drain, for $78.35. I called on any one to bid a less quantity at the same price. I received no bid; therefore going through the usual mode, I said, "Going at $78 35, for 80 rods — once — twice; and after I had said "going," twice, the Misses Smith seemed so excited, and Mr. Kellogg had asked them to bid, that I didn't know but they really meant to bid it in; so I stopped and asked Miss Abby if she wanted to bid; if so, there was an opportunity; if not, I should declare it sold. She said she did not. Mr. Kellogg asked her if he should not bid for her. She told him, no. I declared the property sold to Nelson A. Hardin, and gave him the warranty deed. It was duly lodged in the town clerk's office. Mr Hardin paid me the $78.35, and I paid the money into the town treasury.

Q. You heard the testimony of Miss Julia E. Smith. Allow me to refresh your memory. She says that you said in reply to some question of hers, that "the land was already bargained for." Did you make such a remark?

A. No sir; nothing to that effect, or that could be construed so.

Q. She says that Miss Abby said: "Why, Mr. Andrews, how can you do so wrong?" And that you said in reply, "I have engaged to do it."

A. Nothing of the kind did I say.

Q. Have you stated all to the best of your recollection?

A. Yes sir.

Q. Did you make any remark of this kind: "I shall sell 80 rods west of the drain; it is bargained for at $78.35?"

CROSS-EXAMINATION.79

A. No sir.

CROSS-EXAMINED BY MR. CORNWALL.

Q. When was this writ placed in your hands?

A. I don't remember the day.

Q. Who handed it to you?

A. Guy Samson.

Q. Did he convey it with any instructions?

A. He wanted me to collect the tax as soon as I could as the treasury was in want of money.

Q. Did he give you any special instructions in reference to the tax against the heirs of Hannah H. Smith?

A. No sir.

Q. Did he at any time give you any instructions?

A. He gave me some advice.

Q. Did he at any time give you any special instructions in relation to this tax against the heirs of Hannah H. Smith?

A. I don't understand what you mean.

Q. Did he give you any instructions?

A. I advised with him in regard to the tax.

Q. That doesn't answer my question. Did Mr. Samson give you any instructions in regard to this tax against the heirs of Hannah H. Smith?

A. He directed me to go on and collect it.

Q. Did he instruct you what property to take?

A. He advised me.

Q. Did he instruct you?

A. Well, I don't know whether I would take it as instruction or advice.

Q. What did he say?

JUDGE WALDO. I object to the question.

MR. CORNWALL. The matter is important. The witness commenced by saying this book was put into his hands; and I want to know whether any special instruction was given him. He says he was directed to go on.

JUDGE WALDO. I want to know your object.

MR. CORNWALL. I want to show that arrangements were made between this officer and other officers for the purpose of levying this tax—that it was an unfair scheme on their part.

JUDGE WALDO. Do you claim there was a conspiracy formed for the benefit of the conspirators?

MR. CORNWALL. I claim that there was a scheme for the purpose of harassing and vexing these ladies.

MR. CORNWALL RESUMES HIS CROSS-EXAMINATION.

Q. He directed you to go on and collect the tax. Did he direct you on what property to levy?

A. He told me that if they turned out personal property that in my judgement was sufficient, to take it; if not, he advised me to take real estate.

Q. When was this said to you?

A. Very soon after I called for the tax and they refused.

Q. Did he tell you what real estate to take?

A. No sir.

Q. There were no directions in relation to the meadow land?

A. No sir. He remarked that if I took the meadow land it would probably take a less number of acres. He made that suggestion.

Q. Did he advise you to take the meadow land?

A. No sir.

Q. Did he talk with you more than once about it?

A. Yes, several times.

Q. Anything different from this?

A. No sir.

Q. Did he in any of these conversations direct you to take this land?

A. No sir.

Q. You called upon them on the 18th of March?

A. Yes, I think it was.

Q. And Mr. Brainard went with you?

A. Yes sir.

Q. Did you take him as a witness?

A. Yes.

Q. How came you to take him to this particular place? Were you in the habit of taking him around with you as a witness?

A. No; I don't know that I ever took him any where else.

Q. What time of day did you go there?

A. In the afternoon.

Q. Whom did you find when you went in?

A. Miss Julia and Abby Smith, and Mrs. Kellogg.

Q. Any one else?

A. No sir.

Q. What part of the house did you go into?

A. I went in at the front door, and passed into the south front room, and from that into the back sitting-room. I think it was all opened into one room at that time.

Q. Where did you find these ladies?

A. In the back sitting-room. I think there were folding-doors, open at this time.

Q. You passed through both rooms?

A. Yes.

Q. Did you go into any other part of the house?

A. No sir, not at that time.

Q. Had you been there recently before that?

A. Yes sir.

Q. How long before?

A. Some three or four months.

Q. What parts of the house did you go into at that time?

A. Into the north front room, and into a back room.

Q. The one you spoke of before was the south room?

A. Yes sir.

Q. At this time, on the 18th of March, did you go to the barn?

A. No sir.

Q. Did you go to any other part of the house besides these rooms you have mentioned?

A. No sir.

Q. When you were there three or four months before the 18th of March in the north front room and back room, was that the same back room that you were in on the 18th of March?

A. No sir.

Q. Did you go up stairs?

A. No sir.

Q. Did you go into the kitchen?

A. I don't know what they call the kitchen.

Q. Did you go into any other rooms besides these four rooms?

A. I passed through the house; I don't remember what rooms I passed through.

Q. When was that?

A. The time I mentioned—three or four months before.

Q. Did you go to the barn several times about that time?

A. Twice, I believe.

Q. On this 18th of March, I understand you to say, you asked them to pay the tax?

A. Yes sir.

Q. I believe you said you told them the amount?

A. Yes sir.

Q. During the conversation were both Miss Abby and Julia and Mrs. Kellogg all present?

A. Yes, I think they were.

Q. I understand you to say that when you asked for the tax, some one replied: "Of course we shall not pay it; we have received too much encouragement." Which was it that made the remark?

A. Miss Abby; though they were both talking constantly.

Q. Have you told all that was said about the tax?

A. I think so. The conversation was not all about this particular tax, but about the grievance of not being allowed to vote, and about the letters they had received.

Q. You say you asked them about personal property?

A. I asked them if they had personal property upon which I might levy to satisfy the demand of the law.

Q. Will you swear that this was the language?

A. No sir, I will not swear.

Q. You have testified on this point before?

A. I think I have.

Q. Your testimony before, was before the magistrate?

A. Yes sir.

Q. Did you testify before the magistrate that you asked them i they had any personal property to turn out?

A. Yes sir.

Q. Who replied to that?

A. Both of them, I think.

Q. Are you going to swear to that?

A. Miss Abby was nearest me, and I heard more that she said than the other. I will not swear that they both made the same reply. The reply was that they should have nothing to do with this infamous business.

Q. Did both of them say that?

A. No sir, I think not, but both had something to say.

Q. You asked if they had any personal property to turn out, and one of them said: "No; we shall have nothing to do with this infamous business." Who said that?

A. I think it was Miss Abby.

Q. Who did you say before the magistrate made use of that expression?

A. Miss Abby I guess.

Q. You say both replied. Did Miss Julia say, "No; we shall have nothing to do with this infamous business?"

A. She sustained her sister in this.

Q. Did she say anything?

A. It is difficult to tell.

Q. Then you are not going to say that only one of them said that?

A. No sir.

Q. Is that all you remember?

A. We sat a few minutes and heard them talk about their grievances. That is all I remember about this matter.

Q. Do you say that at that time there was nothing said about their having personal property?

A. I don't understand the question.

Q. Do you mean to say that in that interview there was nothing said about their having personal property?

A. I don't recollect anything. My purpose was to take it if they had any. If they had said anything about it I should have remembered it.

Q. Was anything said about the cows there?

A. No sir. [Correcting himself] There might have been something said about them. I think they told me how bad they felt at having them sold. There was nothing said about their being their property.

Q. Anything said about their furniture?

A. No sir; nothing.

Q. Did you see any personal property there at that time?

A. Their house has some furniture in it.

Q. There is some furniture in it, then?

A. I have always found it so when I have been there.

Q. It is fully furnished, is it not?

A. I believe there is some furniture in the rooms I have been in.

Q. I asked if the rooms were not fully furnished?

A. My ideas on furniture may not conform to other people's ideas.

Q. I asked whether the rooms were not fully furnished?

JUDGE WALDO. What do you mean? What does your question call for? Why not ask the witness what he saw there?

Mr. CORNWALL. I ask if there was any furniture in these rooms, and what it was?

A. I saw some chairs.

Q. What else?

A. A settee.

Q. what else?

A. I don't remember.

Q. Was that all?

A. I believe there were carpets on the floor.

Q. Did you see anything else?

A. I don't know whether there were curtains, or not. There were blinds on the house.

Q. Go on and state what you saw?

A. I have stated.

Q. Was that all?

A. I might have seen other things which I don't remember.

Q. Did you look to see what you could see?

A. I usually have my eyes open to surroundings.

Q. Did you have them open then to surroundings?

A. I think so.

Q. Did you see any pictures there?

A. I have on some occasions.

Q. Did you then?

A. I believe I did.

Q. Did you see any mirrors?

A. I don't recollect.

Q. Don't remember that there was a fine mirror right in front of you?

A. No sir.

Q. Did you at the time of this levy make any further search for property than what you made on this occasion?

A. I have testified on this before.

Q. I don't ask what you have testified. Did you make any further search?

A. I looked at their wagons; and I saw some articles in the sheds as I passed through in April.

Q. What did you see there?

A. I saw some wagons. Mr. Kellogg had a wagon back of the barn backing up floodtrash.

Q. Was it theirs?

A. I couldn't swear it was. There were two or three wagons.

Q. Did you ask Mr Kellogg if it was theirs?

A. No sir; I didn't consider it of sufficient value to make any inquiries about.

Q. Did you make any other search than that?

A. I don't remember that I did.

Q. Did you make any search to see any property except what you couldn't help seeing as you went on the place?

A. No sir, I did not. I didn't open any doors; I made no search to see anything except what I couldn't help seeing.

Q. You testified so to the magistrate?

A. Yes.

Q. Was it about the 8th of January that you made a sale of some cows?

A. Yes, on that day.

Q. How many cows did you sell?

A. Three cows and a heifer.

Q. Were these cows in their possession on the 11th of April?

A. I couldn't tell; I didn't see them.

Q. Did you look for them?

A. They were not in the yard.

Q. Did you look for them?

A. I thought of them as I passed through.

Q. Did you look for them?

A. Well, yes.

Q. Where?

A. In the barn yard.

Q. Any where else?

A. No sir.

Q. Didn't you know they were in their possession?

A. No sir.

Q. Didn't you ask them whether they hadn't got these same cows you had sold before?

A. No sir.

Q. Did you ask them if the property in the house belonged to them?

A. No sir.

Q. Didn't they tell you that it did?

A. No sir, not at that time.

Q. When did they tell you that it was theirs?

A. They had called my attention to some pictures their sister had painted, one time on a previous occasion.

Q. Did you see them?

A. I have seen some of them.

Q. Were the pictures there in April when you were there?

A. I saw some pictures.

Q. How many?

A. I didn't count them.

Q. You have some idea, haven't you?

A. There were a few.

Q. A dozen?

6

A. I shouldn't think there were.

Q. When was your attention called to the pictures?

A. When I went to collect a former tax; in December, probably.

Q. That for which you sold the cows?

A. Yes sir.

Q. Didn't they call your attention to the pictures on the 18th of March?

A. No sir.

Q. Didn't they say to you when you asked them for the tax and they said they shouldn't pay it: "We are in the hands of the town. Here are our cows, and here is our furniture; on what are you going to levy?" Didn't they say this?

A. No sir.

Q. Did they say at that time that they had been advised to put their personal property out of their hands, but that they shouldn't do any such thing?

A. They told me that on the 8th of January when I sold the cows.

Q. Did they tell you that at this time?

A. No sir.

Q. What did they tell you on the 8th of January?

A. They told me that their friends had advised them to put their personal property out of their hands.

Q. Did they say they wouldn't do any such thing?

A. I don't recollect that they did.

Q. Didn't you testify so before?

A. I don't recollect that I did. I don't think I did.

Q. You say you made a levy on the land on the 13th of April. Did you have any other interview between the 18th of March and the 13th of April?

A. It was on the 11th of April, I think.

Q. Did you have any interview between those times?

A. No sir.

Q. Did you between those two dates make any search for personal property?

A. No sir.

Q. On the 11th of April you made a levy on the land; had you no interview with them at that time?

A. I think I saw them as I came back from the meadow-hill, and I notified them.

Q. Did you notify them before you went that you was going to levy on their real-estate?

A. I rang their bell and no one answered. When I came back I called.

Q. Did you see anybody then?

A. Yes.

Q. Was there any interview?

A. They asked me what I was going to levy upon. I told them upon real-estate.

Q. You had made your levy then, hadn't you?

A. I hadn't specified the piece of land.

Q. Had you made a levy at that time?

A. Yes sir.

Q. On the day of the sale, how did you go down to the lot; did you go through their land?

A. I passed through their gate; back through their pasture; north across Mr. Horton's land, and then came back upon this fifteen-acre piece.

Q. Your first entry was on the east side of the meadow land, and the second on the west?

A. Yes.

Q. Where were you for a long time previous to your going down into the meadow?

A. At home.

Q. Did you go directly from your home into the meadow?

A. Yes sir. I might have made some stops.

Q. Did you stop for Mr. Hardin?

A. I stopped and hitched my horse.

Q. How long did you stay?

A. Perhaps 15 minutes. I was expecting Mr. Talcott the surveyor, and waited till he came.

Q. You saw Mr Hardin?

A. Yes.

Q. Did you make any arrangement with him to go down to the sale?

A. Yes, I asked him to go down, and he did go down.

Q. Was there any arrangement between you and Mr. Hardin about his bidding on the land?

A. No sir; none before we went down. He said it was no use for him to go down, as they would bid it in—buy it themselves. I told him he had better go down and see it done.

Q. Did you see Mr. Goslee that morning, the 20th of June?

A. No sir.

Q. Had you seen him within a week?

A. Probably I had.

Q. Do you know?

A. No sir.

Q. Had you at any time made any arrangements with Mr. Goslee as to the costs of the sale?

A. I think I had asked him some questions in regard to it.

Q. Had you arranged with him as to the amount of the costs?

A. No sir.

Q. Had he told you what the costs would be?

A. I had asked him some questions.

Q. Had he told you what the costs would be?

A. No sir.

Q. When did you make up the amount of the costs on this levy?

A. On the day of the sale.

Q. Before or after?

A. Before, of course.

Q. How did you get Mr. Goslee's charges for making the deed?

A. I knew about what he had charged on previous occasions.

Q. Then did you charge at a venture, supposing he would charge that amount?

A. Yes.

Q. What did you put into the costs to Mr. Goslee for drawing the deed?

A. I don't remember the figures.

Q. Have you a memorandum?

A. [Taking out a book] Three dollars.

JUDGE WALDO. The court will understand that I object to anything that transpired after these parties went upon the land. I am aware that one aspect may be admissible and another, not. If there was a conspiracy to aggravate and vex these ladies, it is admissible; but I want the court to understand that I am not consenting to sit here and listen to everything that transpired after these parties went upon the land. That has nothing to do with the trespass upon the land.

[Mr. Cornwall continued cross-examination, questioning witness as to manner, time and place of executing the deed; and then as to the detail of the sale. The first part of the latter testimony was similar to that on the direct examination. For lack of time and space we must omit this, and take up cross-examination further along.]

Q. Did any one bid on that statement? [80 rods west of drain, etc.]

A. Yes, two or three times.

Q. Who bid?

A. Nelson A. Hardin.

Q. What was the next thing he said?

A. I think about this stage of the proceedings, Miss Julia Smith came up.

Q. Did she forbid you selling?

A. She cautioned me that the proceedings were not legal.

Q. Did she say that you must take personal property before real estate?

A. I don't recollect.

Q. Don't you recollect what you said yesterday?

A. I don't recollect that.

Q. Did she say it?

A. I don't know. I think it was said on that day. I don't remember when, though I remember hearing it on the lot.

Q. Did she tell you that she had advised with Mayor Robinson and Mr. Johnson?

A. I think she did.

Q. Didn't she tell you that they had an abundance of personal estate you might take?

A. I think not.

Q. Are you willing to say that she did not?

A. I have no recollection of it.

Q. Are you willing to say she did not say it?

JUDGE WALDO. I object to the question. What more can he say?

MR. CORNWALL. Was not her conversation in a high tone of voice?

A. In a remarkably high tone. I heard some things she said. I was carrying on the sale, and they were talking all the time, but I didn't note down all they said.

Q. What next did you do in regard to the sale?

A. I called on the company for bids. I explained that the property was for sale and that I had had a bid of 80 rods west of the drain. Nobody bid.

Q. Did you say that Miss Smith and party were on the lot before you were?

A. Yes.

Q. They preceded you?

A. Yes.

Q. Didn't they go to you as soon as you came on the lot?

A. No sir.

Q. How far away were they when you got there?

A. Quite a distance, towards the west end, or about mid-way of the lot. They saw us coming on the land at a point near the drain, and they began to turn their team and come towards us.

Q. Is there a path?

A. Yes, a cart path on the north side.

Q. Were they on that cart-path?

A. A part of the time. In turning around they had to drive in the grass.

Q. What did you mean by saying you saw them driving about in the grass? You gave the Court to understand that they were trampling down the grass, when it seems they only touched on the grass as they were obliged to in turning around the team. Isn't that all?

A. They got out of the wagons and came through the grass towards us. Miss Julia got out first, and came to meet me.

Q. Do you say that at that time you had made an offer of the land?

A. I had had a bid. I was brought up to hold my tongue when other people were talking, and I have never got over the habit. So I opened the sale before they got there, as I knew both would be talking together.

Q. Did you mean to sell it before they got there?

A. No sir.

Q. You had had one bidder; why shouldn't you have waited till they got there? Even if they did talk you could have put up their property.

A. I suppose so.

Q. How was the balance of the expenses determined? You put in Mr. Goslee's bill at $3.00; how did you get Mr. Talcott's and his assistants?

A. I had engaged him on previous occasions and knew about what it would be.

Q. How much did you put down for Talcott and his assistants?

A. 86.50.

Q. How long were you down there?

A. Long enough to make the sale, and measure off the land.

Q. How long were you there?

A. I didn't hold a watch in my hand.

Q. I didn't ask anything about a watch. You have some idea as to the time you were there.

A. Probably three quarters of an hour.

Thos. H. L. Talcott, surveyor, was the next witness. His testimony was similar to the preceding. He also testified that all the bidding there was, was before the Misses Smith got there. We will make a few extracts from this testimony on the direct examination by Mr. Goslee, at the point where the Misses Smith had come up.

Q. Did Mr. Kellogg say anything to anybody?

A. He talked to the women; I didn't hear distinctly what he said. He said something to which they replied "No."

Q. Did they ask Mr. Andrews who the bidder was?

A. Yes; he replied, "I have such a bid; you can bid if you want to." They replied, "If you mean to violate the laws you can't compel us to."

Q. Did Mr. Andrews tell them who the bidder was?

A. Yes; he said it was Nelson A. Hardin; at which they said, "Oh, he can't have it! We would rather the lawyers would have the whole of it."

Q. Did Mr. Andrews make the remark—testified to by Miss Julia—that the lot had already been bargained for? Did you hear him make such a remark?

A. No sir, he certainly did not; if he had I should have suggested that he was talking something about which he had no business.

CROSS-EXAMINED BY MR. CORNWALL.

Q. Mr. Andrews didn't tell who the bidder was, did he, when the ladies asked him?

A. He replied "I have had a bid."

Q. He didn't answer their question then. Do you say that these ladies were not present when the sale opened?

A. They were some distance off.

Q. As you had time in your mind to suggest improprieties, didn't you have time to suggest the propriety of waiting till the ladies got there?

A. No sir.

[The rest of this testimony contained nothing new.]

Mr. Arthur M. Brainard was next sworn. His testimony was similar to the preceding. On the cross-examination he testified that nothing was said by the Misses Smith about personal property when he called with Mr. Andrews; that the word "cow" was not mentioned: that nothing was said about furniture; nor about bank-stock, that he remembered. From the cross-examination we make a few extracts.

Q. Did Mr. Andrews ask them if they had any personal property?

A. No sir, not aside from the other question. He asked them if they had any personal property to turn out.

Q. Did you yourself see any personal property there?

A. Well, I saw some rather ancient looking furniture there—some chairs and a lounge I noticed more particularly. The doors were carpeted, I think. I should say the rooms were ordinarily furnished, the same as any one in comfortable circumstances would furnish a house. I didn't take particular notice of any piece of furniture except this lounge, which happened to be in front of me as I sat there.

Q. You spoke of a large mirror when you testified before the justice.

A. I didn't notice it particularly, but there was a large mirror hanging there.

Q. How large?

A. I didn't notice; it was an ordinary mirror.

Q. About how large?

A. Two feet wide and three feet long, perhaps. Not much smaller than that. It had a gilt frame or a wood one. I should think it was gilt.

Q. Did you see property enough there to pay a tax of 50 dollars?

A. No sir; I shouldn't want to take it for the tax and run the risk of it.

Q. If you were collecting a tax you would take it as far as it went?

A. Yes sir.

Q. Did you see any other property except what was in these rooms?

A. No sir.

Q. How came you to go there?

A. Mr. Andrews invited me.

Q. Did he tell you what he wanted you for?

A. Not in particular. He said he was going to Miss Smith's for the tax, and asked me to go.

Q. Did he tell you he wanted you for a witness?

A. I think he did.

Q. Have you stated all the conversation that was had there?

A. All that pertains to the case; all that was said about personal property, and as it was said; the same language that was used, as far as my memory serves me.

Q. Nothing was said about cows?

A. Not in my hearing.

Q. Did you write down what was said?

A. No sir.

Q. When was your attention first called to it after you were there?

A. Well, it was a matter I had thought of considerably It was a novelty to me; I had never been called for any such purpose before.

Q. You had never known of a levy on land?

A. Not in our own place.

Q. Who was there during this conversation?

A The Misses Smith and Mrs. Kellogg. Mr. Lee came in while we were sitting.

Q Did you state to the other court that this call was made on the last of March or the first of April?

A. Not positively. I had no date of it.

Q. Didn't you say before the magistrate that you would not be positive that they did not tell Mr. Andrews that they had personal property?

A. I might have said that I would not swear that they did not say so.

Q. Didn't you say before the magistrate that one of the Misses Smith said: "We thought Mr. Kellogg could hold the cows, but we find on inquiry that he cannot?"

A. I don't remember saying anything of the kind.

Q. Will you swear that you did not?

A. I will not swear, for I might have forgotton it. It is a new idea entirely.

Q Didn't you there say that one of the parties told Mr. Andrews this: "We thought Mr Kellogg could hold the cows, but we find on inquiry that he cannot?"

A. No sir, I did not.

Mr. ―― Brooks of Glastonbury was the next witness. His testimony contained nothing new. He testified, as did the others, that the collector put up the land, and that the bidding was over before Miss Smith's party got up to them.

Mr. Nelson A. Hardin, the man who made the bid on the land, was next called. He also testified that the sale was opened and the bid made before the Misses Smith and party had time to reach them. He made the bid, Said he did not hear Andrews tell Miss Smith that the land was already bargained for. She told him (Andrews) that she forbade the sale; that she had consulted legal counsel, and the sale was unlawful.

Edgar Hale, town clerk of Glastonbury, was next called. Testified that he was one of the assessors of Glastonbury in 1872-3;

that he made up the grand list of the northwest section of the town of Glastonbury for 1873, in which section the Misses Smith live. He gave some testimony in regard to their stock.

Mrs. Juliette Kellogg was next called. Direct examination by Mr. Cornwall.

Q. I suppose you are the person whose name has been mentioned here?

A. Yes sir.

Q. You live in Glastonbury?

A. Yes sir.

Q. In the house of the plaintiff?

A. Yes sir.

Q. I want to call your attention to the interview at the Misses Smith's house, when Mr. Brainard and the collector called. What time was it?

A. In the afternoon.

Q. Do you remember the day of the month?

A. I remember because my attention has been called to it. It was on the 18th of March.

Q. What year?

A. 1874.

Q. Will you state what was said and done there?

A. The collector, Mr. Andrews called with Mr. Brainard. The collector said he had come for the tax. I think he asked them if they had anything to turn out. They told him they should not aid him in doing what they considered wrong. They said they were in the hands of the town, and the town could do with them what they pleased.

Q. Who said that?

A. Miss Abby. Some other conversation followed, and Miss Julia said, "We have been advised to secrete our pictures and the best of our furniture, but we have never done anything underhanded, and we don't mean to." She then said. "There are our cows; we thought Mr. Kellogg could own them, as he had bid them off But our lawyer told us that unless they were driven off the premises they could be taken just the same. So we own them still."

Q. Anything further said about the property?

A. Miss Abby said, "Which will you take—the cows, or the furniture?" He said, "I think I shall take land this time." She asked him what land, and he said he hadn't made up his mind. There was nothing further in relation to that.

Q. As I understand you, Mr. Andrews said he had called for the tax, and wanted to know if they had anything to turn out, at which Miss Abby said, "We shall not aid you to do anything we think is wrong. We are in the hands of the town; they must do as they think best." Now let me call your attention to the occurrence on the meadow on the 20th of June.

A. We started from the house ten minutes before 2. Miss Julia said she must be on the ground as soon as the collector. When we got there we could not find them, and concluded they had gone to some other part of the ground. Then we looked around and saw some men on the meadow-hill, under the walnut trees. They crossed over Mr. Horton's lot. When we saw them they turned around and came back.

Q. You were in the wagon?

A. We were; and we turned around and went back as fast as we could. We were going east. Miss Julia got out as soon as the wagon stopped, and ran towards the collector. He was just coming on the lot. We had just got into the road. She went north-east, and met him before he got across the road. The conversation that passed between them, I could not hear.

Q. Did you hear any portion of it?

A. No sir.

Q. Did you hear her voice speaking to him?

A. Oh yes; but I couldn't hear what she said.

Q. Where were the other parties that came in company with the collector?

A. They were across the road on the south.

Q. If there was any conversation you heard relating to the matter of the tax or the levy, you can state it.

A. I don't know that I heard any of it; not enough to make a connected statement.

Q. You remained sitting in the wagon?

A. I didn't get out of the wagon.

Q. Are you perfectly familiar with the property and furniture in the house of the Misses Smith?

A. Yes sir.

Q. Will you state whether there is property there to any amount?

A. I should think there are as many as twenty pictures in the two south rooms in which the collector and Mr. Brainard were.

Q. What kind of pictures?

A. Paintings.

Q. What else in these rooms?

A. There are two sofas; a mirror that reaches from the ceiling to the floor.

Q. Is there a mirror there that would measure two feet by three?

A. No sir. The one I speak of is nearly three feet wide, and reaches nearly from floor to ceiling. It rests on a marble stand-ard, supported by brackets.

Q. What is the width of the marble?

A. It fills up the space between the two windows. It is the whole width of the glass.

Q. How far does it come out into the room?

A. Over a foot, I should think. It reaches beyond the casings of the two windows. It is a comparatively new glass. They haven't had it over a year.

Q. What is the value of the glass?

A. I believe they paid $90 for it.

Q. What else was there besides the mirror, the pictures, and the two sofas?

A. There were carpets, chairs, tables, curtains. etc.

Q. Is the house large or small?

A. It is a large house, with large rooms.

Q. Were the other parts of the house furnished?

A. Yes sir.

Q. Have you any idea of the value of the furniture?

A. I don't know that I could estimate its value. There are a great many things in the house—very nice beds and bedding; a great quantity of it.

CROSS–QUESTIONED BY JUDGE WALDO.

Q. You say, Mrs. Kellogg, that when Mr. Andrews called with Mr. Brainard, you were present?

A. Yes sir.

Q. And Mr. Andrews first said that he had called for the tax?

A. Yes sir.

Q. Did he tell them what the amount was?

A. I don't recollect.

Q. Do you remember whether he had anything in his hand?

A. Yes, a book.

Q. Should you think it anything like this book?

A. Yes sir.

Q. Did he from that state to them anything except the amount of the tax?

A. I don't recollect. He asked them if they had anything to turn out, and they said they should not do anything to aid the town.

Q. Who was it that first introduced anything about personal property?

A. Miss Julia; she said they had been advised to secrete their pictures and the best of their furniture.

Q. Did she tell by whom?

A. No sir.

Q. What did she refer to?

A. The pictures they had.

Q. Do you know where they got their pictures?

A. They say their sister painted them. I have heard them say so a great many times.

Q. How long have you been in Glastonbury?

A. 17 years.

Q. They spoke of the pictures and the best of the furniture. What was said about the cows?

A. Miss Julia said: " We thought Mr.

Kellogg could own our cows, but our lawyers have said that unless they were driven off the premises we own them still; and she said they could be taken again."

Q. Did she say that their lawyers had advised them that they were their's still? I want you to say whether they didn't say just this; that if the property was not driven off the premises, they could be taken still?

A. The lawyer said they owned them still.

Q. You say that Miss Abby asked which he would take — cows or furniture? Did they state which cows?

A. No sir.

Q. Did they offer to turn out any of the cows, or any particular piece of furniture?

A. No sir. They simply asked which he would take—cows or furniture.

Q. You say there were chairs, tables, lounges, and a mirror which had been bought within a year. Which of the sisters bought the mirror?

A. I supposed they claimed it together.

Q. You say they claimed it as their property. How was it with the furniture? There is one sofa they bought long after Hannah Smith died?

A. Yes.

Q. What else?

A. I don't remember anything else.

Q. Were the carpets new or old?

A. They had them before their mother died.

Q. Do you know anything about the rest of the furniture?

A. Only what they have told me.

Q. You say you started from your house to go to the lot on the 20th of June about ten minutes before 2. How far is the house from the lot?

A. I couldn't say. It took us about five minutes to get there.

Q. How long were you on the lot before you saw these gentlemen on the hill?

A. Half an hour.

Q. If you got to the lot in five minutes, they were under the tree before half-past two?

A. I couldn't say as to that. We were there a long time.

Q. You say the four men with the collector got on the lot before he did. How many minutes before?

A. Not many.

Q. Did you hear the collector put up the land and strike it off?

A. Yes sir.

Mr. CORNWALL. You say you heard the collector set up the lot; was it before or after Miss Julia approached him?

A. It was after. Both Julia and Abby were there before the lot was set up.

Q. You are sure of that?

A. Yes sir.

Miss Julia E. Smith was called again. Her testimony was in regard to the collector's visit on the 18th of March, and the sale of the land on the 20th of June, and was similar to Mrs. Kellogg's. To avoid repetition we will give only parts of it. In speaking of the conversation with the collector on the 18th of March, she said:

I told him we had never acted in an underhand way, but always openly and honestly. When I told him "Here is our furniture," I pointed with my hand, for I meant the whole of it. Then I said, "There are our cows." I told him he had the power to take anything.

Q. Did he state the amount of the tax?

A. I think he did.

Q. You told him you had the furniture and the cows?

A. Yes; I pointed to the furniture; the cows, he could see right out of the window. I said, "There are our cows in the yard; and here is the furniture."

Q. Did he ask you if you owned the property?

A. Oh no; he had no doubt as to that.

Q. How many pictures should you think there were in all?

A. About 30, I should think.

Q. Did these cows belong to you?

A. Certainly; we didn't inherit them from our mother; I raised them myself, eight or ten years ago.

Q. What occurred on the 20th of June?

A. I was afraid I should not get there as soon as the collector, and when I saw the collector coming I ran—and I can run pretty fast. I said right off, "Mr. Andrews, you can't sell this land; it is contrary to law." He replied, "It is already bargained for." Those are the very words. He said it was up for $78.35, and if we wanted to, we could bid more. My sister said, "Why do you do so wrong?" He said, "I have engaged to do it." I said, "You can't oblige us to go contrary to law, if you men break the laws." He said he was going to sell 80 rods west of the drain.

Q. How much is that worth?

A. We could get $2000 (two thousand) dollars in a moment for that eleven acres.

Q. What was the date of his last call?

A. It was on the 11th of April. He said then that he believed he should take land. My sister asked him what land, and he said he hadn't decided.

Q. Did you own bank stock at that time?

A. Yes sir.

CROSS-QUESTIONED BY JUDGE WALDO.

Q. I understand you to say that those pictures were the work of your sister. Which one was it?

A. Laurilla, the middle one.

Q. When did Laurilla die?

A. On the 19th of March, 1857.

Q. Did these pictures all belong to her?

A. Yes sir; she painted them all with her own hand.

Q. Did she make a will?

A. Yes sir.

Q. Was that proved in the court of probate?

A. To be sure it was.

Q. Was there an inventory made?

A. I think not.

Q. Had she any other property than the pictures?

A. She had an equal share with the rest of us jn the property left by our mother, besides some old fashioned furniture which our mother left her when she died.

Q. Did your mother make a will?

A. No sir.

Q. Did you buy any furniture before Laurilla died?

A. I think likely.

Miss Abby H. Smith called. Direct examination by Mr. Cornwall.

Q. Mr. Brainard spoke of a small looking-glass there, two feet by three.

A. There is no such glass there. The large one hung right in front of him; he couldn't help seeing it. There are four of the pictures that are worth $50 apiece; and some of the chairs were six dollars apiece. The carpets are solid Brussels. Anybody would say that they were worth the tax. We expected those carpets would be taken up. Besides, there was hay and grain enough in the barn to pay it; and corn enough in the corn-house, and wood enough in the wood-house, all cut up.

Q. What amount of bedding had you there?

A. There were two rooms close by with beds in them. We have six large feather beds in the house, and six or seven single ones.

Q. Did the collector inquire of you if there was any property there that belonged to the heirs of Hannah H. Smith?

A. He never said anything about the heirs of Hannah H. Smith.

Q. Did he ask you to turn out property as the heirs of Hannah H. Smith?

A. He never mentioned her name. I didn't use the word infamous. No such word was ever used in the house.

CROSS-QUESTIONED BY JUDGE WALDO.

Q. Did your mother tell what furniture should be given to your sister Laurilla?

A. No; she said her "old furniture." She gave it all to her.

Q. You and your sister didn't differ much on that point?

A. We didn't differ on anything; we never differed.

Q. Does this large glass fit in between the windows?

A. Yes, between the moldings of the windows. It is fastened with screws, and is set on a marble standard. We paid $97 for it.

Q. Did you tell Mr. Andrews that the cows belonged to Mr. Kellogg at one time?

A. I don't remember telling him so.

MR. CORNWALL. The cows came back to your yard?

A. Yes, you ought to have seen them. How they did jump up when they got there!

JUDGE WALDO. Did you furnish Mr. Kellogg the money to bid for the cows?

A. Yes sir. I sprang out of the wagon and told him to bid enough to get them all.

Q. Did you tell him that you would take them of him?

A. No, I expected he would keep them.

Q. Was that your intention to have him bid the cows and you furnish the money?

MISS JULIA SMITH. We lent him the money.

MISS ABBY —— [to some remark about both answering.] We answer just alike.

JUDGE WALDO. I think they are alike, and agree· on everything. And I like to hear them, too.

Q. Did Mr. Kellogg ever milk the cows as his own?.

A. No, I don't think he ever owned them; but we meant he should.

Q. Is it strictly honest now for you to get Mr. Kellogg to bid for these cows for you, and then have him own them to keep them from being taxed?

A. Certainly, perfectly honest.

Q. You thought it not honest to put the pictures under cover, and yet you think it honest to prevent paying a tax?

A. Certainly.

MR. CORNWALL. You understand the purport of Judge Waldo's question? Do you think it honest to do anything to prevent paying a tax? Did you have to put anything out of the way?

A. No sir.

[Miss Smith might have replied to the Judge that there is more honor in the person who refuses to pay an unjust tax, and takes steps to prevent such payment, than in the government that subjects her to such a tax against its own declared principles—principles for which it shed much blood and money a century ago, and now refuses to apply to one half the nation. Reporter.]

MR. CORNWALL, to Miss Julia Smith. Mr. Brainard and Mr. Andrews testify that on inquiring if you had any property to turn out, you replied, "No; we shall have nothing to do with this infamous business." Is that correct?

A. No sir; neither of us ever used the word.

Mr. CORNWALL, to Mrs. Kellogg. Did you hear Miss Smith use this expression? *A.* No sir. It is a word I seldom hear; and never hear them use it.

Mr. Henry A. Lee called. Direct examination.

MR. CORNWALL. You are the Mr. Lee who went down in the meadow at the time of the sale?

A. Yes sir.

Q. I want to inquire what knowledge you have in relation to Miss Julia's going to the collector.

A. She was in the team ahead of me. She got there as soon as he did.

Q. Could there have been any bidding before she got there?

A. What little I saw didn't look as though there had.

Q. Was there time for anything to have been done before she got there?

A. I don't know what might have been done in a few minutes. They might have made some arrangements.

Q. I understand you to say that she was there as soon as he?

A. Yes sir.

Mr. Gustavus Kellogg called. Direct examination.

Q. You were down in the meadow at this sale?

A. Yes sir.

Q. Did you see Miss Julia Smith when she went to the collector?

A. Yes sir. She got out of the wagon where I was and went to him.

Q. Was she in the wagon with you?

A. Yes sir.

Q. Where did she meet him?

A. A little south of the road.

Q. Was it as soon as he came on the lot?

A. About the same time. He might have been there a little before her.

Q. Do you know whether there had been any bidding before she got there? Had there been any time to commence the sale?

A. Well, they might have commenced it.

Q. Did you hear what she said to the collector about putting the property up?

A. I heard them sing out, "Anybody to bid less?"

Q. Was that all you heard?

A. Yes; I didn't hear any bidding.

Mr. Andrews the collector re-called.

MR. GOSLEE. You stated in your testimony this: "Miss Abby said to me, 'I want you to understand that when you come for another tax, we shall own no live stock. They will all be Mr. Kellogg's.'" Do you wish to change that testimony?

A. No sir.

MR. CORNWALL. Who was there when Miss Abby said this?

A. Mr. Kellogg and Miss Julia, I think.

Q. Was Mrs Kellogg there?

A. I didn't see her. I went into the house with Mr. Kellogg. No one was in the room. Miss Abby came in very soon; and before we came away, Miss Julia was in.

Extracts from the argument of Judge Waldo, counsel for collector Andrews.

* * * If this property was given by the daughters to the mother, it couldn't have been the mother's property. Now you see it, and now you don't see it. It isn't Hannah H. Smith's estate. Just as if a man having a warrant against Mr. Cornwall should come and levy against my property because he happens to have my name on his list. * * * I don't see what is to be obtained by the prosecution of this suit. It all comes from the movement in society called "woman's rights." They don't need any advice from me; I have never been a lady's man. But I ought to say—perhaps should be proud to say—that I have had an acquaintance with one from their ranks who has brought as much intellect to this movement as any one, and for whom I entertain the highest respect. I have regarded her more than any out of my own family. I sympathize with her. But I have not been, and am not now, strictly a convert to female suffrage. I entertain some doubts about the ballot being extended to every woman in the country. It is now more than a quarter of a century since I lived in a community that thought I was worth a seat in the Legislature. In 1847 I was a member of that body; and there I drew up a bill to protect married women in the rights and use of their separate estates —to protect them against being touched by the creditors of their husbands. That was referred to the judiciary committee. That was the first introduction into the Legislature of Connecticut of woman's rights. I had the good fortune to report it to the house. It went into the house, and I made a speech; but it proved unsuccessful. The next year it met with the same success. I feel that I have a right to say that I have myself always maintained a great abhorrence to those invidious laws that make a distinction between husband and wife in relation to the right each has in the property of the other. The law of 1849, which makes a husband the trustee of the wife's property, and gives him the use during his natural life, I regard as a step forward in the right direction, but not far enough. I have no sympathy with the law that allows a man a hold on the personal property of his wife while it permits him to take away

every cent of property from his wife. I have the greatest abhorrence of the barbarism that sets off a third to the widow, while no such limitation is put upon the husband. And I have no sympathy with the law that prohibits my daughter from disposing of the property I may give her — prevents her from disposing of it without the consent of her husband. Those laws are a blot upon our state, and should be remedied. But is it the object of this suit to effect anything of this kind for these plaintiffs? Did they ever stand in a relation to have any fear from any of these things? The only thing the suit is brought for is to establish the question whether the ladies shall have the right to vote. It seems a great mistake; and those who sympathize with them are making a sad mistake. They are striking at the root of government. What is it that protects them in their rights except the law towards which they are unwilling to pay a single cent? They feel that their property has been trespassed upon, and they come here, occupying the time of your Honor, for three days; occupying these court rooms—taking up public time, and spending public money. And when they are asked to spend a single cent towards the public good, they say, "Hands off!" Why? "Because you don't let us vote," they say. That seems all there is to this case. When I heard them yesterday describing their property, I thought I could fancy them standing before that mirror they so graphically described, and perhaps fostering their self-complacency upon the reflection which it gave back to them. Still, I thought I saw a scowl when they saw the tax-collector coming. Supposing we should all refuse to pay taxes? What would become of us? We should go back to anarchy at once. I think my friends have made a sad mistake. They should use their blandishments to get their real evils removed rather than strive for a good which is no good at all.

[There are several remarkable things in the Judge's argument. In the first place, the conspicuous absence of logic, and in its place considerable talk about women's rights and looking-glass blandishments. In the second place, he appears to have abandoned his original plea—original in a double sense—that these daughters are not the owners of their father's and mother's property, of which they have been the sole and undisputed possessors the last quarter of a century. In the third place, he gives the court to understand that these women have not as good a right to occupy the court room and the Judge's time as the rest of the people for whose benefit these courts are kept up. But the Judge's remark was doubly weak; for while these women have

as indisputable a right to the public's court and judges as any of the rest of the people; in this particular case, their occupancy of the court-room, and of the Judge's time was not their own doing. The case was settled to their satisfaction by the Glastonbury Judge. It was Judge Waldo's own client —the defendant, Andrews, who brought the case to the Court of Common Pleas. In the fourth place—and this, perhaps, is the most remarkable feature of the argument— he states that this suit is brought to establish the question of the right of woman suffrage! Had a woman lawyer made such a statement, it would have been attributed to the natural inability of womankind to use logic. There are several aspects in which this statement can be viewed, and each one seems a little more ludicrous than the other. In the first place, these ladies didn't bring the case here at all; they had to come against their will. If it was brought to prove the right of woman suffrage, collector Andrews is responsible for it, and has a deeper sense of justice than any one has ever given him credit for; though how he was to advance the cause, and on this particular indictment—trespass on land—it is difficult to see. If the Judge's claim is that the case was originally carried into litigation by the plaintiffs for the purpose of proving the right of woman suffrage, it is still as ludicrous as before. The collector trespassed on their land and sold it in violation of law—there being plenty of movable property. First class lawyers pronounced the law to be on their side. They carried it before the Glastonbury Judge, who also decided in their favor. Where does woman suffrage come in? It has no more connection with the case than man suffrage, or Kamschatka has. Reporter.]

A few extracts from the plea of Mr. Goslee of Glastonbury.

Knowing the outrageous slanders of these parties through the public press, my client thought it necessary to take some one with him as a witness of what was said. There was nothing said about personal property; nothing that they could turn out. Now then, if they had said what they say they did, wouldn't he have levied on that property? My friend Mrs. Kellogg says she didn't hear them say so. They have their blandishments. Mrs. Kellogg is the wife of the person who has taken their land. Probably she has talked the matter over with them, and she can only say she didn't hear it. They told Mr. Kellogg that hereafter they should own no live-stock. He was justified in not levying upon the cows—they said they shouldn't own them. As to the other movable property, there was none that could be taken upon this warrant. Supposing there had been? Is there any lawyer here that will advise going into a man's house, or woman's, and taking property? Would the collector have been justified in going into that house and levying upon that furniture and running the risk he would have of taking too much. I should decidedly hate to direct any officer to levy upon household furniture. It isn't true that taxes take the last loaf of bread from the poor man. Certain things are exempt. So far as their property was concerned, he made all the search that was necessary. He saw these old traps lying outside, but nothing was to be obtained; no hay; so far as that was concerned, nobody knew but Mr Kellogg owned it. It seems to me the officer was perfectly justified in neglecting to make any further search. There was no property he could have taken with any safety. Supposing he had gone out of town and levied on Julia Smith's bank stock? Would she have been obliged to pay it? Wouldn't she have brought action against some one? No doubt about that question. He levied his warrant upon the real estate, which no one can question as being the property of the heirs of Hannah H. Smith. I was pleased to see what a time the Judge had in keeping Miss Julia to time. She did want to say a great deal about the visit of the collector on the 11th of April when no one was with him. But she didn't get much opportunity. * * * It is claimed he took too much land. The feeling that Mr. Hardin was the only person able to buy, is unjust. They were all good for $78.00. They all waited for a bid, and no one spoke. These ladies are anxious to be martyrs to this great principle of, I don't know exactly what. I don't know how much they sacrificed on the cows — that is Mr. Kellogg's matter. But when it comes to sacrificing $2,000 for a tax of $70.00, they begin to think that is drawing it pretty strong. I don't know any other way than to do just as the rest of us do—pay. By doing that, they will avoid trouble; and when they come down to the grave—as probably they must, in the course of time—they will probably be attended by many friends who will remember their good deeds. I do think it is too bad that they should end in this way by fighting their native town—fighting the officers of the town where they live. It is a little remarkable that they should do it. It is undoubtedly true that they found it difficult to get any one to take up the case for them.

[There are one or two points worth noticing in the above extracts. Mr. Goslee says that Mrs. Kellogg said she didn't hear them say anything about personal property. He would do well to read the verbatim report of Mrs. Kellogg's testimony, in which she testifies that they said they had been advised to secrete their pictures and the best of their furniture, but should not do so; and furthermore testifies that they stated that they owned the cows still, and asked which they would take—cows, or furniture? He says they had no personal property, and then proceeds to make the remarkable statement that the collector would not have been justified in levying upon it in case they had any, as he would have run the risk of taking too much. Was such an argument ever urged before against levying on personal property? No such fear appears to have actuated these gentlemen in levying on the real estate, for they swung in there with a delightful freedom from all restraint—taking $2,000 worth to pay a tax of $78.00. Mr Goslee makes another noticeable statement. He says no one can question that the property seized was owned by the heirs of Hannah H. Smith. This is an uncalled for cut on Judge Waldo, whose principle plea—or the one he started out to make—was that these good ladies had no jot nor tittle of right to this property —were neither the owners, nor possessors of it. But the contradictions and inconsistences that one meets at every turn and corner where wrong and injustice are upheld, are innumerable. There is an old maxim that one falsehood requires twenty more to back it up.

By way of change and refreshment we will turn to the plea of Mr. Cornwall, counsel for the plaintiffs. Reporter.]

Mr. Cornwall's Plea.

An officer is bound to levy on personal estate. I understand that my friend here is trying to prove that the plaintiffs were not in possession of the property. She swears explicitly, "We were in possession of it. We only gave Mr. Kellogg permission to cut the grass." Didn't she swear that she was in possession?

Judge Waldo. No sir.

Mr. Cornwall. It cannot be seriously claimed here that my clients were not in possession of the property. It is claiming too much to say that Mr. Kellogg was in possession of this property. It is claimed here that there was no personal property there which the officer could take—none belonging to the estate of Hannah H. Smith. On whom did the officer make his demand when he went there? This list says, Hannah H. Smith's heirs — not Hannah H. Smith's estate. Of whom did the collector make the demand when he went to collect this tax? Why, he went direct to Hannah H. Smith's heirs. Who are Hannah H. Smith's heirs? These good ladies. Is there anybody else who can claim heirship here? We have proved here who the heirs are. We have gone back to the father and mother, and come down with the five sisters. These two ladies are the only living heirs of Hannah H. Smith. There has never been any other claimant. There is a decision of the Supreme Court that says when you are to make a levy, you must make a demand of the tax. A demand is absolutely necessary before a levy. This officer says he did make a demand. How did he do it? By going right to the heirs of Hannah H. Smith. If he did not go to Hannah H. Smith's heirs, then his demand was illegal. I don't care which horn of the dilemma my friends take. They have got to be tossed upon one or the other. The tax list is made out to the heirs of Hannah H. Smith, not to the estate of Hannah H. Smith.

JUDGE WALDO. So with the other sisters.

MR. CORNWALL. But they are dead. They are not Hannah H. Smith's heirs after they have gone under ground.

JUDGE WALDO. There was no personal property belonging to that estate of Hannah H. Smith.

MR. CORNWALL. The gentleman makes the point that there was no personal estate of Hannah H. Smith remaining, and there was real estate remaining. But the officer is not levying on the estate of Hannah H. Smith; he is to levy upon the estate of the heirs. The property they put on the list is their property—not the property of Hannah H. Smith. It is *their* property that is to be taken—*their* property that pays the tax. The gentleman says it is the presumption of the law that the collector did his duty. My brother finds fault with these good ladies for striking at the root of all law. He made some sensible remarks a little out side of the case, with reference to the rights of women, in which I shall agree. But I go further than he does. Mr. Goslee says that by reason of the outrageous slanders of my clients, the collector had to take a witness with him. These good ladies had been slandering somebody. Well, we will meet that by and by. I ask the attention of your honor to the facts. In my opening argument this morning, I claimed, and satisfactorily established to the court, I think, that all the proceedings were illegal. That the assessment was void. That was the claim I made. What claim do they set up against the claim I have made in relation to the void assessment and the void return to the town clerk? Absolutely nothing, excepting that they say this evidence is not admissible. Can they show that it is not a void tax? When my friend says these good ladies have nothing to do but to pay their tax, I reply that there is no legal tax.

Haven't they a right to object when there is an illegal claim upon them? The idea is ridiculous that you can't resist an illegal assessment. Here is an illegal assessment, and these ladies have a right to object to paying it. They did object. It ought not to be enforced upon them because it is illegal. And because it may be true that a legal warrant may be issued upon an invalid assessment, that is no reason why they should go forward and pay it. We start with this fact before the court— these ladies objecting to pay an illegal tax. They had a right to object to it. What the gentleman says about these ladies occupying the court and spending the money of the state in resisting this tax, does not apply to this case. They have a perfect right to come here; though in this case, as it happens, they do not come voluntarily. The collector brought them here on this illegal tax. They carried their suit before the magistrate of their own town; and they were willing to let it remain there. But the other side was not. So then, they are here by compulsion. They went before the magistrate because it was their right to do so; and they have the same right to be here. Now this officer has got his warrant on his tax bill against these ladies. Before this, he has levied upon certain property of these ladies, made out against the Hannah H. Smith heirs. They say that made a great deal of noise over the whole country, from one end to the other. Well, it did. This collector thought to himself, "I guess I will make them squeak this time." He was preparing for battle; going to make them do something. He got the thing all fixed up; took a witness with him—a thing he never did before in his life. He went to the house of these ladies with a Mr. Brainard. There is nothing against him except that his memory is bad. It is what he didn't remember that we care about. He goes there fortified with this witness, and sits before a mirror extending from ceiling to floor, and says, "I have come for your tax." Well, they say, "We shall not pay it." It was their right to say so. More than that, I say it was their duty to resist, because the tax was made out of an illegal assessment. He says, "Have you any personal property that you will turn out to pay this tax?" He didn't say, by the way, that he had a tax against Hannah H. Smith's heirs. He asked them if they had any personal property. The officer testifies that they replied, "No; we shall have nothing to do with this infamous business." Then Mr Brainard is brought out. He is going to remember just what the collector wants him to. They didn't go to levy on personal property. Mr. Brainard's testimony runs in the same mould: "Have you got anything to turn out?" "No; we shall have nothing to do with this infamous business." My friend complains because these ladies testify alike; but hear the testimony of Mr. Brainard and the collector. And then he is asked if he saw any property. "We saw some pictures and furniture." But the collector was so overcome in the presence of these ladies that he didn't see that big mirror in front of him. Mr. Brainard's eyes were so nearly closed that he could only see a looking-glass, two by three feet in size, when the only one there was three by seven. Look at the surroundings and see what these parties were there for. It was simply to arrange matters so that they could get an excuse for levying on this land. I ask these parties, "Didn't you inquire of these ladies whether this property belonged to them?" They reply, "No; I didn't inquire as to any particular property." "Didn't you go to the town-clerk's office to inquire about bank stock to the amount of five or six thousand dollars? Didn't you look into the yard to see the cows?" What does he reply? "I didn't see anything except such things as I couldn't help seeing." This is the testimony of an officer whose duty it is by law, to levy upon personal property if it is to be had: an officer going into the presence and on the property of these tax-payers, and swearing here, "I didn't see anything except such things as I couldn't help seeing." Was he doing his duty, when the law requires him to search for property? Did he make a search? Not the least in the world. But on the contrary he was attempting to avoid seeing anything except such things as he couldn't help seeing, and asking the protection of a warrant under such circumstances. Instead of being protected, he ought to be mulcted in a large amount. This man was town-collector, and has been for many years. His proceedings were neither reasonable nor right. If he didn't know himself about the property, then it was his duty to find out. I say that this collector with his warrant has entirely failed in his duty. We have proof of an abundance of personal property there. There is, besides, bank stock to the amount of five or six thousand dollars. The gentleman says that is out of his province. Not at all. An officer may go where his tax-debtor has property. He might have come to Hartford and levied on that bank stock. The law gives him all the latitude of a sheriff in the execution of his duty. Now taking their own testimony, what justification have they shown for doing what they have done? —for levying upon two or three thousand dollars worth of property, and then selling eleven acres of land, proved here to be worth 250 dollars an acre? Is this fair-

ness? or is it a petty scheme for the purpose of bringing these ladies to terms? "Ah," says my brother Goslee, "we have levied on their cows, and we don't want personal property again; but when we come to levy upon two or three thousand dollars worth of real estate, we will bring them to terms." Was it fair in the officer to sell that eleven acres of land under the circumstances he did? Wasn't it in violation of his duty? I say it was. He knew perfectly well that there was only one man there to bid. Besides the collector and this man Hardin—who was to do the bidding—there were only these two, the surveyor and his two assistants. He puts the land up. I don't care what form he took. Mr. Hardin—who is too kindly-disposed—says, "I will take 80 rods from the drain, and pay the tax." That took eleven acres of land. Mr. Hardin knew the value of it, and the collector knew the value. Nobody to bid. I want to know if it was fair. Couldn't he have adjourned the sale to some future time in order to give others an opportunity to bid? On the other side, where were these ladies? O, they had already informed them they shouldn't aid them in doing wrong. They were not there to bid. Ought not the officer to have said, "I will not take that bid for fear some one else would want to bid?" Ought he not to have said, "You all know the value of this land; I will put up an acre." Any one would have taken an acre to pay the tax. No; there was something there that was not right. I say that without any evidence on our part, we might rest this matter right here on the duty of this officer. But we have some testimony. The point is, had these ladies personal property? Did they tender it on the demand of this officer? If they did not tender it, did they not show property sufficient to pay the tax? Didn't they point out property sufficient? Can you have any doubt but what they did? Miss Julia says she doesn't know what tendering means. No one supposes they were to take up a piece of property thrust it in his face and say, "Here, sir, is personal property." But what did they do? What has been proved here that they did do? Why, if ever there was proof of tendering personal property to pay a tax, it has been made in this case. We introduced Mrs. Kellogg. I believe my friends on the other side don't pretend to say that she always testifies and sees everything just as these ladies do. She is a native witness, and a friend of the parties, of course. But who says she is not truthful? Who intimates that she is not to be believed in every word she utters? The individual doesn't exist that dares to say that woman will come before this court and swear to a lie. What does she say? I think her testimony is worth as much as this collector's and Mr. Brainard's put together. She was not there as a witness. She was there accidentally. On the 18th of March Mr. Andrews and Mr. Brainard called. Mr. Andrews said he had called for the tax; asked if they had anything to turn out. Miss Abby said, "We shall not aid you to do anything we think is wrong; but we are in the hands of the town, and they must do as they think best;" or words to that effect. What did she mean by being in the hands of the town? That the town had already seized some of their personal property. They had been advised to secrete their valuable pictures, but they would not do it because they didn't desire to do wrong. Miss Julia said, "We have been advised to secrete our pictures and the best of our furniture, but we shall do no such thing. We have not been dishonest, and don't mean to be." Wasn't that a declaration to this officer and his witness, who didn't hear it, that the pictures and furniture were theirs? And then Miss Julia says, "And there are our cows. We thought Mr. Kellogg could own them as he bid them off, but we have been advised by our counsel that this is not so; they remain in our possession." And now, what? Miss Abby says to the officer, "Which will you take, the cows, or the furniture?" Isn't that a tender of property? or does this woman lie? "Here is our furniture, and here are our cows: which are you going to take?" What did the officer say? "I think I shall take land this time." That is it exactly. That is what he had started upon. He didn't mean to take personal property. He had no idea of it. She asked him what land. He said he hadn't made up his mind. Now how perfectly natural this conversation is testified to by Mrs. Kellogg. Can anybody

believe that that conversation didn't take place, although the officer and Mr. Brainard are not willing to testify to it? The collector had started for a certain purpose, and that was to seize land, consequently he couldn't see anything except what he was obliged to. Does she say anything different on the cross-examination? Not a word. Then we introduced the testimony of these two ladies, and they swear substantially the same thing. I agree that they don't put it in language so explicitly from point to point. Why? I suppose it was because, as they testified, that in listening to testimony that was not true, they became excited. If you were to tell me things that were not true, I should be apt to get excited. The collector and Mr. Brainard had just been testifying to what was not true, and the testimony of these ladies was more or less excited. But whether excited or not, they testify to the same facts that Mrs. Kellogg does. They sustain her testimony entirely. "Why," says Mrs. Kellogg, "if this was not showing property, I don't know what tendering or offering property is." Truly she might say that. "Here are our cows; here is our furniture; which are you going to take?" Well, they say they had no right to take their property because it was exempt by law. But I have never understood that anything that came under the head of personal property was exempt by law. I have always understood, and believe others have, that two things are absolutely certain—death and taxes.

Note—Three suits have arisen from the unjust treatment the Misses Smith recieved at the sale of their land in June, 1974. The first one was before the Glastonbury magistrate, and was decided in their favor. The second one (of which the above is a report) was the collector's appeal from that decision, and was decided against them. The third one,—November, 1876, and in the same court, but with another Judge (McManus)—was decided in their favor. Reporter.

THE END.

American Women: Images and Realities

An Arno Press Collection

[Adams, Charles F., editor]. **Correspondence between John Adams and Mercy Warren Relating to Her "History of the American Revolution," July-August, 1807.** With a new appendix of specimen pages from the **"History."** 1878.

[Arling], Emanie Sachs. **"The Terrible Siren": Victoria Woodhull, (1838-1927).** 1928.

Beard, Mary Ritter. **Woman's Work in Municipalities.** 1915.

Blanc, Madame [Marie Therese de Solms]. **The Condition of Woman in the United States.** 1895.

Bradford, Gamaliel. **Wives.** 1925.

Branagan, Thomas. **The Excellency of the Female Character Vindicated.** 1808.

Breckinridge, Sophonisba P. **Women in the Twentieth Century.** 1933.

Campbell, Helen. **Women Wage-Earners.** 1893.

Coolidge, Mary Roberts. **Why Women Are So.** 1912.

Dall, Caroline H. **The College, the Market, and the Court.** 1867.

[D'Arusmont], Frances Wright. **Life, Letters and Lectures: 1834, 1844.** 1972.

Davis, Almond H. **The Female Preacher, or Memoir of Salome Lincoln.** 1843.

Ellington, George. **The Women of New York.** 1869.

Farnham, Eliza W[oodson]. **Life in Prairie Land.** 1846.

Gage, Matilda Joslyn. **Woman, Church and State.** [1900].

Gilman, Charlotte Perkins. **The Living of Charlotte Perkins Gilman.** 1935.

Groves, Ernest R. **The American Woman.** 1944.

Hale, [Sarah J.] **Manners; or, Happy Homes and Good Society All the Year Round.** 1868.

Higginson, Thomas Wentworth. **Women and the Alphabet.** 1900.

Howe, Julia Ward, editor. **Sex and Education.** 1874.

La Follette, Suzanne. **Concerning Women.** 1926.

Leslie, Eliza. **Miss Leslie's Behaviour Book: A Guide and Manual for Ladies.** 1859.

Livermore, Mary A. **My Story of the War.** 1889.

Logan, Mrs. John A. (Mary S.) **The Part Taken By Women in American History.** 1912.

McGuire, Judith W. (A Lady of Virginia). **Diary of a Southern Refugee, During the War.** 1867.

Mann, Herman. **The Female Review: Life of Deborah Sampson.** 1866.

Meyer, Annie Nathan, editor.**Woman's Work in America.** 1891.

Myerson, Abraham. **The Nervous Housewife.** 1927.

Parsons, Elsie Clews. **The Old-Fashioned Woman.** 1913.

Porter, Sarah Harvey. **The Life and Times of Anne Royall.** 1909.

Pruette, Lorine. **Women and Leisure: A Study of Social Waste.** 1924.

Salmon, Lucy Maynard. **Domestic Service.** 1897.

Sanger, William W. **The History of Prostitution.** 1859.

Smith, Julia E. **Abby Smith and Her Cows.** 1877.

Spencer, Anna Garlin. **Woman's Share in Social Culture.** 1913.

Sprague, William Forrest. **Women and the West.** 1940.

Stanton, Elizabeth Cady. **The Woman's Bible** Parts I and II. 1895/1898.

Stewart, Mrs. Eliza Daniel. **Memories of the Crusade.** 1889.

Todd, John. **Woman's Rights.** 1867. [Dodge, Mary A.] (Gail Hamilton, pseud.) **Woman's Wrongs.** 1868.

Van Rensselaer, Mrs. John King. **The Goede Vrouw of Mana-ha-ta.** 1898.

Velazquez, Loreta Janeta. **The Woman in Battle.** 1876.

Vietor, Agnes C., editor. **A Woman's Quest: The Life of Marie E. Zakrzewska, M.D.** 1924.

Woodbury, Helen L. Sumner. **Equal Suffrage.** 1909.

Young, Ann Eliza. **Wife No. 19.** 1875.